There is
a Season

There is
a Season

A Search for Meaning

Eugene S. Geissler

Introduction by John S. Dunne, C.S.C.
Art by Sarah Geissler

Ave Maria Press
Notre Dame, Indiana

921
635

ACKNOWLEDGMENTS

To my wife; to Kathleen, Mary-and-John, Sarah, Sheila, Molly, Nora, Peter, Teresa, Eileen, Michael, Annie, Margaret, Agnes, Maura, Mark, Justin—all for contributions peculiarly their own; to Albert Bauman, O.S.B.—for his special contribution; and to Kenneth Peters and Charles E. Jones—for theirs.

Library of Congress Catalog Card Number: 69-17337
© 1970 by Ave Maria Press. All rights reserved
Clothbound edition published February 1969
ISBN 0-87793-022-8

Manufactured in the United States of America

To

the Governs

and

the Pleasants

with whom

we have been

friends together

There is a season for everything
and a time for every purpose under heaven

A time to be born
and a time to die
A time to plant
and a time to reap
A time to hurt
and a time to heal
A time to tear down
and a time to build up
A time to cry
and a time to laugh
A time to cast away stones
and a time to gather stones together
A time to embrace
and a time to refrain from embracing
A time to gain
and a time to lose
A time to keep
and a time to throw away
A time to rend
and a time to sew
A time to speak
and a time to be silent
A time to love
and a time to hate
A time for war
and a time for peace

What has a man to show for his trying?
What is the meaning of it all?

according to
Ecclesiastes 3:1-9

Preface

WHY does anybody write anything?

This question occurs to me as I try to give an account of what I have done in this book. What have I written and why have I written it?

After thinking about it a long time, I would like to identify this book as a search for meaning. It is a part of one man's search for the meaning of life.

We are all very much aware and engaged these days in this search for meaning. An explanation of life worthy of man is the thing after all which haunts us about life and converts life itself into a pursuit for meaning.

I have searched the meaning on the level of everyman, for everyman has at his disposal and in his experience the things I write about, and it is on this basis of universality that I present the events and details which I have selected. The framework might be considered remotely "autobiographical," but I would feel misinterpreted if this were accounted as important or more than a vehicle for the search.

Most of this book is the 1960s, but some of it goes back briefly to the 1850s, to 1900, to 1917, and the following intervening years. It goes back this way because this is the way a man's life goes back into the past. Any man's life. Every man has a history, a particular, peculiar history of his own, and this history in its essentials touches and repeats at poignant points of its experience the universal experience of mankind.

Why does anybody write anything? Because he wants to share something with another, and that something has significance for them both. He hopes for a moment of truth, a moment of community which leaves both of them enriched, however slightly, but enriched.

To be acceptable as enriching experience, this shared something must always be the truth, not the whole truth perhaps, but the truth. Furthermore, it has to be real life truth, for man today is not satisfied with less, and on a certain level of communication this real life truth is personal revelation and in turn involves and reveals the person of the other.

What I have written about my children, they have passed for publication when they might have vetoed it. They passed it, I think, because it is the truth (without being all of it), and because it did all happen some few years ago by now—and for a young person a few years ago is ancient history.

As for the rest, the Lord bless us all!

Eugene S. Geissler

Contents

Introduction

THERE is a season, the author tells us, for confronting life, and that season occurs, as one would expect, during one's adolescence. The season returns, however, when the wheel of life comes round again during the adolescence of one's children. Even the ordinary man, according to this extraordinary book, is called upon to face life again and to search for meaning once more when his children begin to do so. The story of a life, from this viewpoint, starts with the youth of a man's father, goes through his own youth, and carries into the youth of his children.

The book begins, accordingly, with the story of the author's father. There is a touch of Genesis about the tale as he tells it. The love affair between his father and mother is told with the simplicity of the story of Jacob and Rachel. There is a touch of the New Testament in the account of his father's death, how his father died in his strength, in his mid-thirties, like Christ. The chapter describing this, "A Thimble Full of Tall Tale," is one of the best in the book. The story of how his eldest brother took his father's place as head of the family is important on the first turning of the wheel of life. The father died in the spring of life; the years of the ascendancy of the eldest brother were "Thirty Years of Summer," and the season of the eldest brother's death was the autumn of life. There is indeed "a time to be born and a time to die," as it says in Ecclesiastes, and this theme continues into the second part of the book.

The story of the daughter who died in earliest childhood, the one child who died in the author's large family (sixteen children), occupies the whole second part of the book. It is not traditional to tell the story of a child of one's own who died in infancy. The English poet John Donne, for example, had some twelve children, six of whom died during childhood; also he wrote some of the most famous funeral poetry in the language; but he never wrote a poem about the death of one of his own children. There is little precedent to help and there is undoubtedly much emotional difficulty to hinder a man trying to describe his own child's death. The author shows no striving for any kind of literary effect here but only a striving, by coming back to it again and again, to assimilate an experience which was one of the most difficult and most central of his life. The experience of an infant's death is one of the most universal of human experiences, but for all its universality one of the most unsung. Here is an unpolished but very stirring meditation upon it.

So far the story is a tale of three deaths, a father's, a brother's and a daughter's. Now it becomes a tale of many lives. Part Three is about Kitty, Mary, Sarah and Sheila, the author's eldest daughters. The reader can verify what is said about Sarah by comparing it with her art in this book and her "Art Notes" at the end. The title of the opening chapter of this part, "Art and Life Are Where You Find Them" is also from her. The images which arise out of a person's feelings are "art where you find it," and the feelings out of which they arise are "life where you find it." The author begins to tell in this part how he learned from his own children, from their art and their life. The two essential conditions for the further education of a father, one can see from this, are that the father encourage his children to give free imaginative expression to their feelings and that he be willing to learn new things from his encounter with their feelings and the expression they give to them.

If it is not traditional to write about the death of an infant as the author did in Part Two, it is equally untraditional to write about the lives of older children, especially after they have reached adolescence, as the author does in the last two parts of this book. The last part tells of Molly, Nora and Peter, the next eldest daughters and the eldest son, who was fourteen at the time of writing three years ago. The reason that the author does these two untraditional things and omits the conventional thing —the description of one's very young children—is that he is telling about the things from which a father learns the most. The death of a child is one; the emancipation of a child is another. When one's children reach adolescence, they cease to be as simple and understandable as they once were when they were very young. The author's wisdom is to see this not only as a stage in the education of his children but also as a stage in his own education, a still unfinished stage. "The circle of life," he says, "grows wider and wider." In the end he speaks of the world of the father "vanishing" or at least "diminishing" in the life of his children and of fatherhood vanishing or diminishing in his own life—a remarkable piece of self-honesty, for one would be tempted to conclude from the book as a whole that fatherhood was the entire meaning of the author's life.

One can see from this that fatherhood does not become a kind of myth in this book. The author does not make it into a solution to the problem of death, an immortality achieved by having children who survive one's personal lifetime. The first two parts, dealing with the death of father, brother and daughter, do not offer any easy answer to death. The last two parts, dealing with the lives of the eldest daughters and the eldest son, do not picture the children as a mere extension of the father, destined to survive him, but on the contrary envision them as worlds in themselves, full of their own riches. The circle of life becomes indeed wider and wider.

This simple and marvelous book shows how wide and encompassing the circle of life can become in a day when death seems to reign in the world at large. It seems to say that there is a richness in the simple human roles of husband and wife, father and mother, son and daughter, brother and sister, that makes life worthwhile in a modern world which is impoverished in spirit.

John S. Dunne, C.S.C.

14

Part I

1
Love Affair

THE TWO VALLEYS on each side of the row of hills finally converge, where the hills abruptly end, in a wide expanse of prairie. The row of hills runs miles and miles back and was in those days covered thick and heavy with a stand of oak and maple, ash and elm, poplar and birch. Only where it ended abruptly on the edge of the prairie, there it was pine. Nothing else was abrupt, but round and rolling, low and high.

In the 1850s when the settlers first came to this part of Wisconsin both the hills and the valleys were all woods, and the first roads running up from the prairie followed the crooked paths of least resistance up the valleys. Each settler went a little beyond the last one to his piece of land homesteaded from the government—rich land from a generous government, as it turned out. In other places, like southern Indiana, for instance, settlers were not so lucky. The land turned out poor and the settlers, like Abe Lincoln's father, moved on to better land. But here the land was good and the same last names are still on the mailboxes.

Even my own grandfather, who first built on the sandy loam on the edge of the prairie by the pine bluff, later moved up the valley into the heavy woods and the clay loam soil. He never moved again, but lived there with his wife for sixty years before he died. They had nine children by 1880, the youngest of whom was Henry. It was a rugged life; every winter, besides fighting the weather, they felled two more acres of timber and chopped it up for firewood, fence posts, or sawed it into lumber for building. During the summer, besides working the farm, they grubbed out the stubborn stumps and broke the new land. All of it was hard human labor with human hands—except what two horses could contribute.

By the time Henry was twenty-one in 1900, much of the land in the lower part of the valley was cleared, and the view was sometimes a mile long looking up or down the road, but looking in the other direction it ran quickly into the hills and the edge of the woods.

But in 1900 when Henry was twenty-one, he was in love with a girl from the valley across the hills and his thoughts were on different things. The other valley was only a mile away over the hills, but three quarters of that was woods, and if a man was not careful he could even get lost in it, especially coming back at night from courting his girl.

This other valley leading up from the other side

of the pine bluff at the edge of the prairie was in some ways different. It was settled later and most of the people were Lutherans. Of all the things that might happen to Henry from the Catholic valley on the one side of the hills nothing could match his falling in love with a Lutheran girl from the other valley on the other side of the hills. That mile of long and lordly woods was a long mile indeed.

It was this other valley that had the public school; it was this other valley that had two or three little Protestant churches in as many miles; it was this other valley that had the remarks about no meat on Fridays and about priests that didn't marry, and things like that.

But for Henry this other valley also had Matilda. Matilda was, like Henry, twenty-one years old in 1900. Because her valley was settled later, she was the oldest of eight children in her family, not the youngest like Henry.

Though the peoples of the valleys didn't mix much, they did meet at the country store, the creamery, the saloon which were common to them both at the edge of the prairie where the roads converged. It was also here that the one Catholic church with its high wooden steeple, ball and cross dominated the countryside, and next to it the commanding three-story, four-classroom Catholic schoolhouse. The grand affair of the year was the annual parish picnic to which people came from miles around. Lutherans were invited to this money-raising affair as well as the Catholics. It was there in 1899 that Henry met Matilda.

Nobody introduced them. They merely found

themselves next to each other in the chicken dinner line. Somebody pushed Henry, maybe just to get things started, and this made Henry bump into Matilda. Their eyes met briefly when she turned around, because of the bump. Henry of course blushed a little because he was an innocent bystander to the whole affair. He guffawed and goofed a bit to cover the whole thing up. Matilda found it funny enough to laugh a little and look at him again. It was plainly hard to get a conversation going in those days with a new girl you didn't know.

Henry, watching her from behind, was beginning to like little things about her. For a while he studied the white of her neck between her ear and the collar of her dress, but it was hard to get going. Sitting down next to her at one of the tables didn't help the conversation either at first, except that at least there was something to do now. He passed her the fried chicken boldly, and she said the first word which was a thank you. Henry liked the sound of it and the way she said it, and said a thank you in his turn when she passed him the gravy. And so with a couple of thank yous they got going bit by bit.

By the time dinner was over Henry knew that she was from the Lutheran valley, and Matilda knew he was from the Catholic valley. For the day, though, they were young enough to forget about it. After all, Henry was a handsome boy, and Matilda, besides being pretty, had just enough spark and sass about her to keep Henry interested. He took her around to some of the stands after dinner and even won her a box of candy on a raffle ticket. At the end of the day they went home up their separate valleys the way they came.

But they never forgot each other again, and by the time a year rolled around without seeing each other, they found themselves looking for each other at the same church affair in 1900. This time when their eyes met words came easily. It is part of the mystery of sex, love and life that, sometimes at least, a bond builds up between two without their being together at all.

Thus it was that Henry began courting Matilda across that long mile of hills, and got lost one night in the woods coming home in the dark. He had "to roll stones all night to keep the wolves away," he said. Where he got the stones he didn't say, but Henry made it home safely in the morning. For a lesson he had to work all day without sleep.

Before the year was out Henry and Matilda were married in the Catholic church and the two valleys never were so far apart again as they were before that.

Henry and Matilda had eight children of which I was the sixth, born in 1913.

2
A Thimble Full
of Tall Tale

CHRIST DIED in the spring when every tomorrow is full of power. Because Christ did all things perfectly, he died in the spring when he was young and strong. I do not think that Christ did anything haphazardly, or that he did anything less that he could do more, or that whatever he did lacked ultimate significance. If he died at thirty, thirty-three, or thirty-five, it was because that age represented the high point. In the flush of life in the flush of spring—strong man going out in the strong of the year—that was an ultimate choice. To die at twenty is to die before full possession of self; it is premature. To die at fifty is to die after full possession of self; it is anticlimactic. But to die in the middle thirties is to die in full possession, on top of the hill, where all men can see. Then, if I be lifted up on top of the hill, then surely will I draw all things to myself.

My father, Henry, died in the spring when he was young and strong. That's how I know. Is there any other way to know anything for sure? My father died in the spring when things begin to live again. He died young like Christ in his middle thirties. When the old die, there is only so much to die; they have laid down most of their life long ago. Little by little after the middle thirties they start to lay it down. My father died strong; not willingly like Christ perhaps (though I have willed his willingness often for him), but in his strength, not wasted by disease or old age but in his prime without any wasting away. "As strong as any man in the valley," they said, "and half again as strong as any." This they told me over and over again as I was growing up in the valley, and my father began to take shape and to draw me to himself because he died when he was young and strong, in the spring. . . .

Spring is Christ making everything green. Spring is Christ going down into the tomb and pushing life out of the earth. Spring is the power of Christ let loose in the world. Christ is a tall tale of love let loose upon the earth in spring.

Two things mattered. The first is that the one man who laid down his life young and strong in the spring, picked it up again the very same spring. No time lost. One day the earth was dark with the last of dead winter, and rain fell on the tomb. The next day the Easter Christ is making everything green. I've seen it myself. The grass in the spring and the bursting forth out of the earth is one great green alleluia. Christ is a thimble full of tall tale told in the spring, a short tall tale: a good man was killed and rose from the dead as he said. That's all.

The second thing that mattered was that someone believed it, a group of friends believed it; the tall tale was good news to them. Was that equally important as the first? Remember the parable about Dives and Lazarus? Christ himself said that "even if a man came back from the dead they wouldn't believe." He needed somebody to believe, he needed a whole group to believe. If nobody believed and shared it with others who believed, it would come to naught. The coming back from the dead would be shortlived if nobody believed; it would come to naught in a day without a believing community.

I was only four years old when my father died, and it didn't mean that much. A child is a presence that is there; that's all a child is to begin with, a presence in the presence of others to be enlarged, a little presence among the big to be filled out. Through my eyes of two and three and four, I scarcely remembered my father—only a few dramatic incidents: once on a hay load high, a giant looking down at me little on the ground; and another time my hanging on to both his legs at the knees, and most of him above me; and a third time, made to sit along the wall in the dining room with my brothers, by the stern power of his voice over me. Nothing much to go on, a few little pieces of life.

And a few little pieces of dying and death: the parish priest in horse and buggy coming down the lane to get him ready; our kneeling in prayer for the dying at his bedside; and my lifting the sheet that covered his naked body on a stretcher in the parlor (prime-of-life-man laid out flat and long). I was only four years old then.

A few little pieces of life and death to go by; a few little pieces to build into an image, a few little pieces to make stretch into a continuity. No, not really. Not really at all. There is another way to know something for sure, and that is to believe. There is what I know myself about my father and there is what I know from others and from Christ.

The community kept him alive for me; they kept him before my eyes. Because he died young and strong, they couldn't forget him. Because they remembered him in his prime, they wanted him to live. Strong as any man and again half as strong as any. How can such a man be dead? They continually resurrected him for me till his presence grew and I grew with it into a man. They filled him out for me, not by the many things they said about him, but by that thimble full of tall tale, and by the way they believed in his strength. And eventually I believed—in his strength and in mine.

So in the end there are four of us: Christ, my father, the community and I. And the marvel of it is that there was such a man, that there is such a man, and that we are one together because in him we are identified. We all have learned from each other, about each other, and we all live one by the other and we are grateful to each other. What is lacking in one is made up by the other, and we all contribute to the filling out.

My father is fifty years dead this very day (as I write these last paragraphs), and my children on that score were happy to go to Mass with me; they were impressed that I should remember so long, or perhaps that I should have already gone so far beyond my father in years. But this I know, that a father's life is short among men—give or take a generation or two—unless he becomes part of the one tall tale.

3
My Oldest
Brother and I

THE STORY of my oldest brother begins when my father, Henry, the youngest of his mother's nine children, died. I was four. The year was 1917.

My oldest brother, the first of eight children—one of them still to be born—was sixteen. It was spring, but the spring of his life was cut short, and he was tossed like a green stick into the summer fire. Along with the next older brother and sister, fourteen and twelve, he was pulled out of school to work the farm and raise the family. At sixteen he was in the eighth grade, would have graduated in a few months, and would have quite distinguished himself by doing so. One of his favorite stories was to tell about the lad in the eighth grade who delighted in saying about himself that he was third highest in the class—there being only three in the class.

Overnight my oldest brother became the new father of the family, an acquired relationship and responsibility which I don't think he ever quite relinquished for the rest of his life. Even through his own marrying, raising a family of his own, and becoming a grandfather, he continued to be a kind of father to his brothers and sisters. All his life, he rejoiced with them as a father in their successes and grieved with them in their troubles, though he couldn't, like any other father, always solve their difficulties for them. But he was always sympathetic, understanding, patient, and compassionate. I see now the value of these human virtues: they render a human help far above mere power, wealth, and any material goods. And so few people have them. I used to think it was almost necessary to be poor to have them, so that if you would give anything to another there was only self to give. But now I know that it has something to do with loving people and being open to them.

When my mother, Matilda, died some years later —having often been sick and for a long time not in good health—what I remember most are the tears that ran down the face of my oldest brother at her funeral. The impact was not that he was a man of calloused hand and hard muscle and the tears contradicted him, but that this kind and gentle big brother of mine should be suffering so before my very eyes.

Perhaps I know from my oldest brother what a father should be like—a mixture of masculine and feminine, strong and gentle, firm and kind, fatherly and motherly both.

Through the early years of his apprenticeship in fatherhood he had his trials and frustrations with the rest of us, though at the time I suppose I wouldn't have been aware of it. Are children ever aware of these things? I remember once when I was asked to do something, nothing arbitrary, to help with the milking maybe, I said no. He started over to where I was; I walked away. He quickened his pace and I began to run. Soon we were both running. We were in a field of clover by now, and when I couldn't run anymore I dropped down into the clover barely ahead of him still. By then I knew I had it coming. If he had picked me up and shaken me, or hit me, or even kicked me, I am sure I would have considered it no more than elementary justice —and probably not have remembered it these forty-fifty years. Instead, he stood above me for a moment only—a tall tower of strength outlined against the evening sky—and then walked away without word or deed.

For a long time the incident remained a mystery to me. It still does. He might have been angry, though this was not one of his traits, but all the more a mystery if he was. Except that now I know that the big man, the strong man, the mature man, at 16 or 61, does not use his strength, does not feel the need to use his strength, against the small, the weak and the immature.

I remember another time when we were getting older, another brother and I were playing hard ball in the yard, and my oldest brother, earnestly going after something or other, walked right between us, and quite accidentally—though not without some negligence on our part—got the baseball squarely on the side of the jaw. It took him by surprise. I thought for a moment that it staggered him a bit. He should have been very angry with us and though he did say something this time, it was very mild indeed: "You should be more careful; you could hurt somebody."

And then there was the time of the big snow-storm, when even the horses got stuck. It was Sunday and my oldest brother, family man of the house, excused us all from going to Mass. But he would go, he said. I can still see him being swallowed up in the wind and the flurry only a short distance from the house, and for three hours the little ones, including myself, walked back and forth to the window wondering if he'd make it there and back. He had three miles to go each way. I can still hear the shout that went up from the little ones, faces pressed against the window, as the form of their tall brother, who represented the family at Mass that day, began to take shape through the snow. His scarf, which was around his neck when he left was now across his hat and ears and tied under his chin. He walked sideways to give his back to the wind. His face looked like worn leather and his frozen rubber boots made noise like pieces of oak wood on the floor when he stepped into the house.

In 1927, at the age of 26, my oldest brother married and moved on to a rented farm some few miles from home. We still saw a lot of him in those days because we helped him with his farm work. His first baby was born during the Al Smith campaign and named Alfred, the first of the new generation. He was born at home. After a day or so, maybe it was only the next day, my oldest brother came to pick up the cradle which for many years now had been stored "on top of the chicken coop." It was a cradle homemade by my father when my oldest brother was born. So now we got it down for my oldest brother's firstborn. But what I remember most was my oldest brother's complaint that "you can't be very anxious to see the new baby because you haven't been over yet." It made no great impression on me then—he smiled when he said it—but when I in my turn began having a family many years later, I often thought of it. Just for this once my oldest brother was looking from us unfeeling and inexperienced younger ones for the response which is usually given by people made sensitive with experience. He was only twelve years older than I but it might as well have been a hundred.

When I reflect upon this time of my growing up, from four to fourteen and beyond to eighteen, I marvel how things held together for this family of eight children. It was my oldest brother (and the next oldest brother and sister) who reared and provided for the rest in place of parents. And what I see as I look back is considerable personal freedom: freedom from rules, freedom from punishments, freedom even from being told what to do. The only discipline I see is that which grew out of the need to help each other and to live together in peace. For the time, place, and people involved it seemed enough. And because there were no parents it was easy to break with some of the old ways. We were the first to have electricity in the home, the first to have a tractor, the first to send anybody to high school, the first to go to college out of the valley. Eventually my next older and next younger brother became priests, the first of the 75-year old parish. I seem sometimes to realize from this that parents can be too much "present" for their children's good as well as too little.

4
Thirty Years
of Summer

THIS is how it was in those days. Men were like horses in harness. Summers were long but not as long as a summer day from dawn to dusk in the fields. Those who worked the earth in those days knew what a day's work was, and how much a man could do in a day.

My oldest brother knew summer well. Most of his life was summer because summers not only were long and hot but also hard. Sun and sweat bleached out his workshirt except where the suspenders went down from his shoulders and crossed in the middle of his back. Sometimes there was only one suspender, like an uncrossed cross, and then you could really tell. I think it was the work—and perhaps the worry of getting it all done—that made him say toward the end: "It's been a good life, but I wouldn't want to live it over again." In the evenings he often fell asleep where he sat from just tiredness. A good life, he said, but once was enough. A good life! The main note was always a positive one, like when I got my first car and he said to me: "Now you have a place for your money."

In 1929, two years after marrying, my oldest brother bought a farm sixteen miles away from home—a farm past another town in "Protestant country." After that we saw less of him. It was a flat farm and had a trout stream running through it. Much of the land was still full of stumps and never broken to the plow. It was now the life of a pioneer all over again for my oldest brother opening up his land. Hard work was his constant companion. The earth is a hard taskmaster, especially for those who want to make something of her. I helped him a few times to dynamite stumps and grub roots out of the soil, and then pile them up and burn them in preparation for breaking the land.

To this day, I like to think of myself on that pine-stump farm with him, listening to his philosophizing about land and life, catching a glimpse of his insights into work and love and providence. He was to me the one man who "saw heaven in a grain of sand," and God in every human being. That is why a younger brother, or even a stranger or any teenager, could spend a day with him dynamiting stumps and bury at the end of the day his old self in one of the stump holes. His innate human sympathy encompassed everyone.

This accounts partly for his being elected town clerk against the incumbent of twenty-four years. In "Protestant country" he gained the reputation of being "the best Christian you could ever meet." As long as he was there he was never again opposed for this elective office.

Nights could be lonely, however, on the "frontier." That is when my oldest brother would entertain with the fiddle, which he learned to play from his father and which was part of his light side as I remember him in this time of his life. I don't think he ever played it for himself alone, but enjoyed playing it for others. His hands together were almost as big as the fiddle, and I marveled how the very large and hard-worked fingers, which in the daytime knew stumps and stubbornness, could in the evening manipulate a combination of strings and bow for joy and music. He always smiled as he played. It seems to me he played mostly in the winter, but I remember one evening, he was induced to play the fiddle, though it was summer. There was a number —"Devil's Dream," I think, I don't remember exactly—during which he asked the children to pay attention not so much to the music as to the silver butt end of the bow. Throughout the number it made a continuous and graceful figure "8". I imagined him a little boy, in his turn sitting many years earlier at his father's elbow, watching that same figure "8" in the same way.

He was ten years on this flat-level, pine-stump farm with the trout stream running through it. The rest of his family of two sons and two daughters was born there, and he achieved a place of love and respect among the people. His children attended the public school of the district. Because he was town clerk, he was also the school clerk. In the winters, the teacher roomed and boarded at his house. For their religious instruction he took his own children eight miles to the parish church in town on weekends.

But he was never quite satisfied with what he called the "light" land, though he left it broken to the plow and better than he found it.

When there was a chance to buy a place in the valley of his youth he bought it, across the road from the home place, halfway up the rolling hill toward the Lutherans. He never tired repeating how "you can't beat this kind of soil anywhere"—heavy, dark, and deep like a secret. Maybe there was better soil elsewhere but he didn't know about it. What he had now in the home valley was for him the best, and it overlooked the valley and the farm of his father, across the road on the other side, now operated by his brother. It was there he had first fallen heir to his father's mantle and was initiated before his time into the long duties of father and husbandman.

Here in the valley where his father had labored, and his grandfather had homesteaded from the government, he lived out the last twenty years of his life.

His high regard for land made him a good husbandman. He knew how to pick up a handful of dirt and talk about it with reverence. Christ had said, "My father is a husbandman," and this he knew too. He was the first in the valley, with the help of the county agent, to follow a program of contour farming. The rolling hills were washing away. There were ditches in the land. It took some courage in a place where it had not been done before to build fences on the bias, to leave in permanent pasture hilltops which had once been grubbed out and broken for tillage in great heat and sweat, and to plow the hillsides not straight up and down but roundabout in a crooked circle. Though it had never before been done in the valley, he did it, and it was a good thing to do for the land. I remember his walking me around and explaining to me the principle of it. "Everyone of those furrows," I remember his saying, "is now like a rain barrel instead of a downspout."

Here too he ran for the office of town clerk in the new township, was elected and for nineteen years until his death was a good public servant. It meant sweating out the tax roll every year; it meant issuing tavern licenses; it meant being on the school board;

it meant endless trips. . . . Added to the six previous years of service in the other township, he was town clerk for a quarter of a century. Eventually, he bought himself a pair of glasses at the dime store for the close work involved.

Here also he first became a grandfather. He was surprised at the many congratulations he received on the birth of his first grandchild. "More than when I became a father," he said. He loved his grandchildren with a great love as perhaps only a grandfather really can, and this particular grandfather's paternal love had been growing, with an early start, for two generations. In return they took out a lease on his lap.

His oldest daughter became a nun, and that pleased him too.

The last time my oldest brother "sat" with his grandchildren, a week before his death, he couldn't really stay awake anymore and so he fell asleep in his weariness, which also turned out this time to be his sickness. The oldest of the six children he was sitting for, herself nine, lovingly covered and cared for him, and then beside him kept his vigil for him until her parents came home. It was like the closing of a circle.

He had five days between the diagnosis and the operation from which he would never regain consciousness. He who never had been sick a day in his life and had a good chance to recover, yet treated these five days as his last. He said goodbye to many, he made a last will and testament, he instructed his wife about a number of things, together they went to the parish church daily. He had never missed a

Sunday Mass in his life and always received Communion, but five days in a row was something special.

The last time he received was an hour before the operation. The evening before, fully conscious, he had been given Extreme Unction. He had gone to confession. It was in character and in keeping with his life to be prepared for death, and though such a blessed ending is not to be presumed upon, it is proof again that the Lord has a penchant for staying with his friends, as St. John says in his gospel: "Having loved his own—he loved them to the end."

The pastor was not satisfied with my attempt to gloss over the loss of this man with: "You know, of course, there is no need to mourn the passing of such a man!" or some such thing. I believed every word of it, but the longtime pastor could only feel very human about it: "Some people you feel very close to . . . and get to know very well and. . . ."

5
I Go Before
You Into Galilee

MY OLDEST BROTHER is dead in the fall, not quite winter yet.

His last days were the beginning of September. This man of sixty—all his life close to the earth—would have been in sharp tune with the dying but sensitive glory about him. In Wisconsin in the fall, the shadows are long and colorful, and so would have been the long thoughts of this man of sixty. He would have known that part of the glory of fall is its dying.

It is not quite winter yet. It is not quite time yet to tune the fiddle and make your own music while the earth still lives. It is good to have learned from your father to play the fiddle against the winter when the earth is dead. For the present, it is still a fall month, and the man of sixty knows from the harmony of the thousand familiar sights and sounds about him that it is not time yet to play the fiddle. He sings instead the sad-happy song of his season.

I wonder who will play the fiddle this winter now that my oldest brother is dead in the fall.

As I ride up the valley of my fathers between the rolling hills, I see again the horizons we shared together, my oldest brother and I—as indeed all of us brothers had shared, for it was the home valley. He was the first to leave the valley before he returned to it again. Now he is the first of us to have left the valley for good.

This man, my oldest brother, my second father, is dead now, he is no more. On the outside his life was little and humble. The universality of the common man is there; all the ordinary things out of which the common man weaves for himself the simple, factual record of his having lived are there: birth, school, work, suffering, tears, smiles, love, marriage, children—grandchildren if a man is lucky—death. Perhaps the name "Reinhard" was uncommon and not much else.

Yet he *was* different beyond his name. I know. A few others knew him better, I am sure, yet there remains something to me: I always wanted to be like him, and though I failed in this, I am the moth that looked into the light. There, amid all the ordinariness of his life, I beheld him as exceptional.

I keep thinking how wrong he was when he said during those suddenly ill days that if he did die only his wife would miss him. His own children, he said, had their own families, and their own cares. He did not even mention other possibilities. Only his wife would miss him. The minute I heard it I knew how wrong he was. It wasn't that the news of his death was so sudden. It was what it did to me.

Yet it would not be worth the saying it, except to myself, if it were something just between my oldest brother and myself. It is rather that what he was to me he was to many other people like myself who needed help of various kinds.

The "people" are not persons far and wide who have seen him like a man on TV, or heard him like a voice on radio, or perhaps read him as they would a man's thoughts in a book. No, he moved a common man among the common people, perhaps a little uncommon for this age in this, that he lived where he was born and was buried where he lived, among his parents and grandparents. Draw a circle with a radius of fifteen miles and you encompass all the area of his labors, and with but rare exception the extent of his movement. In this bit of a circumscribed world the things the common people said about this common man were firsthand things like these, and I heard them over and over again: "No better man ever lived." "He was such a good man!" "He was always helping someone else." "He worried about everybody." "I don't remember ever so much as an unkind word." "If he didn't get to heaven the rest of us don't have a chance." "A lot of people are going to miss Ren." ("Ren" or "Reinie" is what the people called him.) "Praise God for such a man!"

Do you know such a man too! In so many ways he was so ordinary that there must be many like him. He was not singled out in any special way by either events or deeds. He did nothing heroic. His death caused no great stir. He moved in a small world and for the rest nobody ever heard of him.

Yet there is something I feel certain about; I know for sure: God loved him from the beginning and from the beginning blessed him. If you ask me what it means "to be predestined by God" or "to be one of God's elect," why, I think I know the answer now (which I never could understand from philosophy and theology) from the way my oldest brother lived and died. God blessed him from the beginning; he endowed him with great meekness and made him his brother's keeper; he planted the love of neighbor deep in his heart with a special concern for the weak, the lonely, and the little; he gave him a simple and abiding love of his law that I don't think he ever knowingly transgressed. He was like a man out of the Scriptures. Psalm 1 fits him well, and the beatitudes, St. Paul and St. James: "Blessed is the man who delights in the law of the Lord . . . Blessed are the meek . . . He who loves his neighbor has fulfilled the law . . . To feed widows and orphans. . . ."

Perhaps he did not know the Apocalypse well enough to close his life with "Come, Lord Jesus," but after the anointing of the sick and Holy Viaticum within the last hour of his last lucid moments, he said to his wife in his simple way: "I am ready now."

Death is a go-between, and it is necessary to be friends with death. The crowning glory of life is to make friends with death and at the proper moment to embrace him—like Christ the cross—at the right moment to say, however it comes, "I am ready," "I give up my life," "Into thy hands, O Lord." It is not the end but the big beginning. It is the third birthday of the Christian: into the world, into the church, into eternal life.

Because I truly believe he understood these things, his death was suddenly more like a sorrow-joy to me. The example of his life was like a light still shining. Though I had not been with him much or seen him much in a quarter of a century, my first impression of his death was a great empty space before me that he had filled. I always knew what he would be thinking; when there was trouble I knew what he would say, but he did not need to be near to say it. He was like a man always there no matter where he was. Suddenly I realized that this hadn't really changed with his dying.

So after but a little while I dried my eyes and had no need to grieve again for him.

I was anxious to see the body he left behind and the face so often wet with the sweat of country work. It was a dear face to me, even without the life in it. Here was the man who had been a brother to me, a father to me, and a friend to me—as he had been indeed to many, and it was the being it to many that raised him to a level above the ordinary. He had managed within his small circle to be everybody's father and friend and brother, and the happiness of it is, he will continue to be.

I go before you into Galilee; there you shall see me again.

Part II

IN HIM WAS LIFE
AND THIS LIFE
WAS THE LIGHT
OF MEN

6
Annie of Happy Memory

A NNE MARY, our eleventh child, is dead.

I sit here and think of all the little children that parents have ever lost to early death, and I hesitate, even more than I have ever hesitated, to write about a little child. I hesitate standing in the shadows, as I have hesitated in the warm light, because children in all that they are from the hand of God and our own hands—innocent, undefiled, irresistible, fragile, an impossible prodigious promise spoken into the thin morning air—elude our words and sidestep our courage and leave us but the safety of silent wonder. I have sometimes thought that except for the security of divine life given to them in baptism, I would hesitate to breathe even a word about their existence before they assumed at least the substantiality of a two-year-old.

But Annie is dead in her innocence after but a year and a bit more of natural life and nothing can harm her anymore—not even words that fail to do her justice.

We've had a baby at our house continuously for fifteen years and about each one in turn mother would say, "This is the best one yet." If it did not mark, in fact, progress in the evolution of the species, it did mark progress in our own attitudes and capacities so that by the time Annie arrived she really was, not just to mother but to all twelve of us, every sweet, holy, and superlative thing mother ever whispered into our willing ears about her. And in Annie's case, dead in the splendor of her baptismal innocence (I like repeating this basic fact about her) nothing said of her heretofore or hereafter was and ever will be an overstatement. Annie was and is a blessing on earth as she is in heaven—in heaven of God and on earth of happy memory.

She belonged, as no baby in our house ever has, to everybody, to mother most of all, but also to little two-and-a-half-year-old Michael. He teased Annie a great deal, practically sitting on her in the walker. We often thought he would hurt her, but Annie never thought so, and would play with the big plastic crucifix around his neck which he found one day somewhere in the house and indicated to his father by a strange kind of language to hang around his neck. This his father did after making a hole through it with the electric drill big enough for a roughneck chain. It really was too big a crucifix for a little boy—more like a bishop's—but it did appeal to Annie, and I never see it on Michael now without thinking of how Annie liked to play with it.

She belonged also to Eileen, the four-year-old who

would throw toys back into Annie's playpen as fast as Annie could throw them out. She would scold Annie for not knowing better, but Annie's little grin always disarmed her enough to remind her it was a game they were playing. The main thing about Eileen's relationship with Annie, though, was that Annie always had something to give Eileen; it was attention. This was, in fact, one reason for Annie's popularity: She was always interested in everybody in the house and everyone could get a smile out of Annie. I've seen Eileen, ninth from one end of the family and third from the other, go over to Annie's playpen when things weren't going so well and get all the attention she needed. Subconsciously, she misses Annie a great deal, and her face lights up at the sound of Annie's name.

And Teresa too, the five-year-old, the biggest of the preschoolers. If she would agree to sit in a big chair and not try to get up with her, mother would sometimes put Annie in her arms to hold for awhile. If there was anything wrong with the world for a five-year-old, it all passed away in the glory of getting to hold Annie. She sometimes fed Annie too, her cereal or her banana. Even when it came to eating Annie never did those contrary things most babies do, like spitting it out at you or spraying your face with it. And mother would insist that "God never made a more perfect baby than Annie."

It would seem too bold a thing to say all these wonderful things about Annie's never letting drop one unhappy memory in her life, if she were still alive. But since she died in her innocence a father can say it boldly—without the fear of ever having to retract—and everyone who knew Annie intimately agrees and feels no least hurt, nor envy, nor jealousy. Teresa knows she was Annie's special friend and the feeling, Teresa knows, was mutual.

It is something everyone of us knows.

Now, as for Peter, six-and-a-half-year-old-boy, who might just bump into a baby sister on his way to a bicycle ride with no more than an, "Oh, golly, Annie, what are you doing here?" broke many a winter monotony by pushing Annie around the house in the walker at running speed. I had my doubts about it more than once and said so. But my doubts were an ineffective deterrent because Annie loved it so. Peter would slip himself into the handle frame right behind the walker and with a strong firm hold on the very thing itself would go as fast as he could, which was pretty fast. (I had bought him a pair of tennis shoes for Christmas to cut down on the noise. A side effect was that it speeded him up and things came out about even in the end.)

It was a kind of a figure "8" he did with her, around the center counter in the kitchen and through a door for a circle in the living room. The round trip was maybe a hundred feet and Annie's hair would fly back and sometimes her head too as her feet went up out of balance. The thrill of a roller coaster might well have been old stuff to Annie later in life. The closest thing Annie ever came to being annoyed with anybody was with Peter whenever he would stop to catch up on his breath.

In the course of her young life Peter had made a cross for Annie out of some small scraps of trim left over one day from his father's working on the bedroom wing. It drew from Annie more sighs of **fascination** than of reverence, and she was always willing again and again to be distracted by it on the dressing table. It looked good to us beside her in her coffin and we buried it with her, a genuine product of a young boy's love for his little sister.

I must say something about Nora too, because all her life Nora has wanted to be ahead of her age. It never was good enough for Nora to be doing, for instance what a six-year-old does, when she was six years old. She really was tailor-made to be the oldest child in the family, so capable she is, but in a large family lines must sometimes be drawn somewhere, and the line on taking Annie out of her playpen or out of her walker without help from someone older, and certainly without permission, was drawn this side of Nora. Nora did not appreciate this, of course, and I am not ready to say just how often the letter of the law escaped her; it is certainly an extenuating circumstance to have been reached up to by that irresistible Annie. At any rate, Annie repaid Nora for each of her transgressions with the utmost of warmth and delight. She let the sun of her innocence shine on both sides of any drawn line, on the permitted and unpermitted alike.

And now that Annie is gone I must confess to an indulgent forgiveness toward Nora for having experienced Annie the way she did. And because Annie's new and enlightened understanding of the situation will now come to the help of parent and child alike, I expect for Nora a hundredfold reward from having, unilaterally, ministered to little Annie's wishes —the symbolic cup of cold water.

And how about Molly, Sheila, Sarah, helpful ages nine, ten, eleven, Annie's ever willing servants? Of most happy memory, Annie is to everyone of them. They had their "turns" feeding her, getting her up, entertaining her, praising and thanking God for her. Annie loved them all without ever giving the least impression of spreading herself thin to go around. Maybe all little girls are like this, but Annie had a special knack for it, perhaps because she had so many close friends from the very beginning of her days. I do not remember one single instance when any one of these three was not glad to drop what she was doing to take care of Annie, and the eyes of all them shine with a new splendor as I look into them now, for having known Annie. Molly had lovingly given her a crucifix she herself had won at school. This is the other thing, along with Peter's cross, we buried with her.

Mary, twelve years old, was mother's mainstay in the care of Annie, and had given more of herself and more of her time to Annie than anyone else in the family after mother. And she gave it most kindly, her own needs, at the age of twelve, and Annie's at the age of one, by a marvelous plan of nature, coinciding. Amid the growing pains of life, Mary received for her many selfless ministrations, the recognition and status of which a twelve-year-old sometimes stands in need. It was a happy relationship.

It is one of those unbelievable things in life that Annie should have died a premature death, within reach of all of us, including Mary, in the very midst of us almost, surrounded by love, many willing pairs of hands in the house. It could only be that God loved her still more than we did.

Then there is Kathleen too, age sixteen, touching upon maturity. What are her memories of Annie? With this age it is a little harder to say exactly, or even to be inclined to say. They are more like grown-ups who mean to keep their feelings to themselves. Busyness and preoccupations sometimes come between themselves and human values, but where Annie was concerned there were no secrets. Annie on the changing table upstairs would delight Kathleen getting her up, and Kathleen would delight Annie so that there would be a conversation going on something like this:

"Trying to get away from me, are you?"

"Whee!"

"Now, Annie, don't be so funny."

"Whee!"

"You're just perfect, Annie."

"(Am I really?)"

"Just too perfect, Annie."

The repetition marked the point where words failed and the mystery of the child was overwhelming.

I cannot say for sure, but I think that Kathleen truly understands a little something already, because of Annie, about God's great gift to women: the joys and sorrows of motherhood.

I do not think that I can speak for mother. Her joy of Annie, I am sure, is too many fathoms deep for me. And I do not mean that I am just the father here. A baby and its mother, and a mother and her baby, live by a force of nature a common life of their own. It is a common life firmly knit and inter-woven (what goes on between them is a shuttlecock weaving a golden cloth) and I do not think words have yet been written, or ever shall be, to take the measure of true mother love. It is part of a great mystery because it reflects God's love for us.

We say "God the Father" so easily, forgetting that there is no sex in God and that God is mother too. Think for a moment of those tremendous feminine virtues, in women who are true to their nature—even outside of marriage and parenthood: sympathy, compassion, tenderness, mercy, patience, peace, joy, forgiveness, fidelity, loyalty . . . all reflecting in a way the high regard and deep concern of "person" that is elemental to loving someone else for purely himself, for his own sake, for what he is—which women know how to do best of all. And think of these qualities too as developed and present in a very special way in the true mother toward her own child and I think you may get an insight into God the Father that will reward the effort a hundredfold.

Mother says she never picked up Annie or laid her down without a prayer of some kind to the Father of all of us, to the Blessed Mother, to the Holy Spirit, to Jesus or to one of the saints—a prayer of praise or thanksgiving for so great a gift as Annie, a prayer of humble petition that she always be kept pure, and innocent, and holy, for she was in mother's arms a child of God without spot or blemish. Perhaps, taking her as he did was the only way possible to answer this mother's prayer.

The joy of the mother in this her child was immense and the mother's tears are, believe me, bittersweet tears of sorrow-joy. In no other heart, except the heart of God, is Annie of more happy memory.

For myself I think I knew Annie more through her mother and the others than directly. Father was, in a way, but waiting his turn; her needs and wishes would grow man-size in due time. Springtime was coming and when the family in the annual exodus from confinement to freedom moved outdoors again, father would be king. Among other things, Annie would want her turn with father on the tractor, ploughing the garden or some such thing. There are many things in our haphazard country place that a little child can join in if her father will but let her. Though this would be tomorrow, father anticipated it happily.

Not all was anticipation, however. One grand evening when father's heart was light and the music was on, most of the family sitting around quietly in the various parts of the L-shaped living room—and lo and behold! nobody holding Annie—father picked her up and as he has with all of them at one time or another did a little dance with her. To keep from flying away perhaps on the turns she hugged close to father's shoulder, her little soft face burrowed into father's swarthy neck. She was smiling, her mother said, and only her eyes moved.

First of all, the joy of her being and her baptism, and then perhaps in a special way too this dance with her—these her father keeps for a happy memory of Annie.

Just the other night in answer to a question from one of the children, mother and I tried to explain that if God had chosen to take any of the others instead there would have been bound to be some shadow of regret. There would be something to remember to bother us during the long night, a time to remember when we had to correct and even punish, a time when we would have been irritated and impatient, at least a moment of frustration or complaint, not just ourselves but everyone in the family could surely think of a time when they might have acted more charitably. Not only that, the shadow would also lay upon the dead. There would have been a time to wonder about, some bit of recalcitrance and stubbornness, some bit of anger and self-will, some evidence of sin and Satan at work. And the memory, always happy at least in this that by the love of God they existed, would not be so totally a happy one.

The first Mass after the death of Annie on Good Friday was the Easter Vigil Mass. Our hearts were full to breaking and our grief ran over. It might have come to us at a less "auspicious" Mass as well. I mention this here because it fits in here—one of those moments of insight that open up a whole new world. Mother and I both saw at the same time, I think, for she nudged me and pointed to it in her missal. It was in the prayer immediately after the consecration of the wine, the prayer that offers the victim to God: "Wherefore, O Lord, we thy servants . . . offer to thy excellent majesty, of thy gifts and presents, a pure victim, a holy victim, an immaculate victim . . ."

The victim offered is Christ, of course, but through baptism the life of Christ was in Annie and after that sin had not touched her, nor any evil, neither from within, nor as far as we could know from without. She was the one pure and immaculate thing that we possessed. God had taken her and ours was the privilege to offer her, and I think we both did and I doubt there shall ever be a Mass when we shall not do so again. This above all will become the Annie of happy memory: the pure and spotless Annie, worthy through the merits of Jesus Christ, to be a clean offering to the Father of us all.

7
The Day of
the Long Night

ANNIE died about nine in the evening. Her mother was at church. It was Good Friday. I held Annie in my arms, tight to me, in the back seat of the police car. We had called for an ambulance. Her body still warmed mine on the way to the hospital, but she was already dead.

I found mother in church praying and there I told her. The priest came out of the confessional and quietly reminded her that this was also the day of the Blessed Mother's great sorrow. And he said to praise God to have been so singularly chosen to stand beside his Mother.

After awhile I said to mother we must hurry home; the other children need us. It rallied mother, and we went home. I called out for the oldest, but there was no answer. I called again, louder. Still no answer. I shuddered at the thoughts that came to my mind. Death had found our house tonight, and I was afraid.

I ran upstairs. I stopped halfway up to call again, and then I heard the praying. The six oldest were gathered in the biggest bedroom to say the rosary.

The police had come back to say that Annie was dead, and to ask how did it happen, what was her name, what was her father's name, how many brothers and sisters did she have. Except for the spelling of one of the names the account the children gave came out very accurate in the paper. It was better than I could have done. Death was a stranger in our house and I could not take my eyes away from him. After the police left, the children had gone upstairs to say the rosary.

I opened the door and asked mother to go into the bedroom. The children kept on praying. Some of them were crying as they prayed. When they saw us they seemed to cry the more.

Mother spoke a few words and they stopped. Many times mother had made them listen and now they were glad to listen. "Children, it is God's will that Annie died. This is what your father and I want for all of you. That you do God's will and go to heaven. Annie is with God. Let us try and be happy. It is a blessing." And then mother cried. It was a quiet, little cry. Not the big cry.

I called some friends: Annie's godparents, and some of the closest neighbors. And one of the men who had seen us in church and knew us well brought the pastor out after the confessions.

The hospital called to ask which funeral home to send the body to. We talked this over together. One of our neighbors said that she thought birth and death belonged in the home. And the pastor suggested that there was a special blessing if the priest came to the home for the body the day of the funeral.

We called the hospital back. . . . But on Easter Sunday we wanted the body brought to the house and the funeral would be from the home. It was a consoling decision our good friends helped us make. We began to look forward to Annie's homecoming.

After the pastor left, our friends stayed on. When I said to mother we should go to bed, it was hard to get up and go to bed. Our friends did not leave us, and it was hard to think of leaving our friends. It was hard to think of going to bed.

The same dark night the searchlight and siren had pierced lay before us. It was hard to think of going away from the light of the living room. The bedroom is for the night, a dark place. The face of darkness is the face of death.

All through the night he was with us, and we with him. I saw him in all the dark corners. He was in the howl of the hounds passing, this time of year, under our windows. He was in the big cry of the mother.

He listened to our praying. He listened to the things we said to each other about him. And in between, during the painful silences, he sat on a throne in the center of our bedroom.

Would he ever leave us again? No, he would never leave us again. Did we want him to leave us? Death was a gate through which Annie had gone and if we wanted any contact with Annie. . . . I groaned to think of having to make friends with death. I groaned in the night again and again at having to make friends with death.

Everything within me resisted my going to sleep. And I dared not put on the light. The dark of night is the time to make friends with death. There was no alternative. A light could only interrupt temporarily the dialogue with death.

I began to blame myself. I had casually waved to her as I was going into the basement and when I came up not long after she was dead. . . . But the pastor had said that this is the one thing you must not do, blame yourself.

I planned to ask the children to pray for a miracle of resurrection when Annie came back to the house on Easter Sunday. . . . But then I was afraid to; God knew what was best for Annie and us.

And I began to doubt that baptism was enough for a child to be saved; she had done not one free deed to earn eternal life. . . . But all eternal life is a gift. Through the faith of her parents and the Christian community she was baptized. Through the merits of Christ she is a saint.

And I groaned again that death was here and that there was no way to eternal life except through death. I wanted to get up now and throw him out of the room and be rid of him. Annie had been such a dear child. He could at least let little children alone.

Why? Why? Why? I had heard the inevitable question from others and now I had grievously to answer it for myself. . . . I recalled Job throwing himself naked on the ground: "The Lord gave and the Lord has taken away."

The answers were all rote answers, lip-learned years ago out of a living context, but now I repeated them; I repeated them again and again to myself in a dumb confession of faith.

Mother asked me couldn't I sleep, and I said no, I can't sleep. The night was a year of nights already long. I said I hoped that she could sleep, but she only said that she would pray to Annie that I might sleep. And I groaned again that a night could be so long.

It was but the first of many favors Annie would grant her mother. The father slept and by this mother knew, by the sure light of a woman's faith, that God is good and Christ is God and Annie lives.

I awoke clumsily to the smallest, merest, speck of sunshine in the highest corner of the east window and for one quick second, like a crack in death's armor, it seemed to me that there was nothing wrong with the new day. It had only been a dream. And then I groaned again to remember.

I told mother about this and she said that she was glad I was able to fall asleep. She had not slept at all, she said, but she was glad that Annie had helped her father fall asleep.

The window began to fill with spring sunshine and by some great grace it was like a scroll unfolding the beginning of the gospel of St. John that we said so many times at Mass. The very same I have wondered about being repeated so often, might not more variety be better. . . ? But now I know why it can never be repeated too often. Now I even know why St. John belabors the point, to answer the one question that matters, the question men ask themselves in the dark of night, the question men seek an answer to in the company of death.

> In the beginning was the Word,
> And the Word was with God;
> And the Word was God.
> He was in the beginning with God.
> All things were made through him,
> And without him was made nothing that has
> been made.
> In him was life,
> And the life was the light of men.
> And the light shines in the darkness
> And the darkness grasped it not.

The long night had yet many days to go, maybe it would never end, but it is true, sweetly true, that he who had found our house in the night has become the friend who has visited us in the day.

At the heart of the mystery of death lies this great truth, what else is there to live for? What other way is there to enter into eternal life?

8
Postscript:
Three Years Later

IT IS exactly three years ago today that our Annie died accidentally at the age of fourteen months. I was in the basement, just below Annie when she died, and that's where I first heard the desperate cries for help from some of the older ones. A parent is but seldom, if ever, mistaken about what the cries of his children mean. Before going into the basement, I had waved at her; she had smiled at me, and twenty minutes later I held her dead in my arms. Three years ago it was a Good Friday. This year the day is a Tuesday, not Good Friday anymore. It is a Tuesday in spring, a new spring.

She died in her high chair, and on the night that she died, my good neighbor and I took the high chair, in which she died, and the playpen in which she lived, down into the basement out of sight, and there we left them. The playpen found its way up again when the new baby came and had need of it, but not the high chair.

There it stood in the basement in an undetermined, insoluble way—an old wooden high chair we had acquired secondhand, and ten of our children had used. I worked around it for a long time, but the children, especially the boys—their attention glued to the project in hand—began to push it around and to climb on it to reach high things. Peter had, after all, seen the whole thing very clearly when mother and I awakened him the morning after Annie's death and told him. He was six then. His comment was spontaneous: "Gee, she didn't have to wait very long to see God!" Just that much, nothing more and nothing less. For Peter this conviction has always been sufficient. I am sure he still believes in it as he expressed it then. In fact, with him the thing rather ended there. Faith comes easier to children than to grown-ups.

So, one day, when the tray broke under the blows of his carpentry in the basement and fell off the high chair, I knew somehow that I had mended it for the last time. I took the broken tray to the burning place—as we call it—and tossed it into the fire, because it seemed the logical thing to do. I watched the flames lick into the corners of it. From the very beginning I thought I would someday have to burn the high chair just the way it was, all of it at once, but it was one of those things I could never decide about—how, where, and when. I waited around for something to happen, for something to decide for me; I waited for time to do its work.

It wasn't long after that, that the arms and the back came off under similar circumstances, and like going down a road I had been down before, I took these too, with less labor this time, to the burning place. Finally, in the fever of creative activity in the basement the month before Christmas last, there weren't enough working places to go around. One of the children suggested that I quickly improvise a table on top of what was left of the high chair. That I did. It served the new purpose well and continues to be of service in its new capacity.

About the time I think I have made up with it or forgotten, I see it before me again—what's left of it. I see it, and it strikes me again squarely between the eyes, but each time more tenderly, I think. I suppose I shall one day make up completely with this thing that marks a yet unfinished history. Mother but seldom goes into the basement. She has, I am sure, some other measuring stick for her growth out of the darkness into the light. As for me, it is a long time ago by now, since my good neighbor helped me down the steps with the high chair.

The baby mother was carrying when Annie died, is herself two and a half now. Margaret is her name. She didn't take Annie's place. Nobody could do that! But already she has praised God on earth twice as long as Annie, and delighted all of us with her own special wiles and her own incomparable magic. She never knew Annie. (As I say this, I recall the fact from Scripture about the "new king over Egypt, that knew not Joseph," and what a difference it made for God's chosen people.) But we'll try to tell her about Annie, though it can never be the same as having known her. There is an age gap between this two and half year old Margaret and five year old Michael that is considerably bridged by Margaret's precociousness. Perhaps in time only the parents will know that the gap is there.

Little Agnes, also come since Annie, is a year old. She "plies her little trade" daily before God and her circle of family friends. It is about the way it was with Annie, more than a dozen friends from the very beginning, and all of them her willing servants. Characteristically, she is "the best one yet"—except for Annie, maybe.

One thing I know better about little Agnes than any of the others: what it is to hold a baby alive in my arms at night, listening at length to the rhythm of her breathing in the dark, conscious even of the tick, tick, tick of her heart against me. She hasn't been a good baby and has had us up a lot at night. When mother was nursing her there wasn't much I could do, but after that—well, I shall never again not prize highly the feel of a live child in my arms after having held Annie dead in my arms. I think of it often as I hold Agnes. Sometimes my arms have already begun to ache, and so I am reminded to put her down.

As time goes on, we are ever more certain that God's in his heaven—because Annie is there too. "The day will come," Father Mathis had said, "when you will count her death as a blessing." The fact is, we already do. We celebrate Annie's birthday into heaven with Mass and a special dinner—complete with her baptismal candle, white table cloth, and all. The neighbor lady means it when she says, "I envy you having your own saint in heaven." Mother says that of course she is our saint; we are all she ever knew. On account of it, mother wields a golden wand, and I, I sometimes feel like a spiritual King Midas: my prayers turn things into "gold."

I have come to think of the Apostles Creed as Annie's prayer, because since she never grew up to say it herself I have fallen into the duty of saying it for her, not that she needs it anymore, but because it was her parents' faith in the things of the Apostles Creed that brought her to baptism and a new life in the first place. This saying the Creed in her name first began on a dismal day shortly after her death. I was alone in the car going to Chicago; the road stretched out before me, endlessly it seemed. It was almost like being nowhere because it seemed so far to somewhere. Into this nowhere, this emptiness around me, Annie—once more dead in my arms—intruded herself and I groaned in grief to myself above the roar of the motor. This was not untypical for some months after her death to have it all coming back to me with a bang. But this was more intense than anything before or since, so that I felt overwhelmed: sweat broke out upon my forehead and I was miserably alone. For reasons unknown to me, I began to say the Apostles Creed. The doom and darkness dissipated before me, and it has been "Annie's prayer" ever since. It is also my Midas touch. I added it to the dinner prayers one evening because the one of the children with the stubbornest streak in the house had a terrible mad on. It was almost like a test case for the prayer. By the end of the prayer the stubborn one had quietly come around, and peace had been unbelievably restored. It would be but a coincidence, except that it happens so often.

Another good neighbor read some things from Peguy to me one evening last year. That he did so showed his confidence in my recovery, I think. The excerpt was mainly about fathers, how they of all people cannot escape this world, and in it was this paragraph, ever so true: "Nothing happens, nothing historical, is a matter of indifference to him. Fathers suffer in every event. They suffer everywhere. They alone have exhausted, can boast of having exhausted, temporal suffering. Those who have not had a sick child do not know what sickness is. Those who have not lost a child, who have not seen their child dead, do not know what mourning is. And do not know what death is."

Annie's grave is in the cemetery across the road from our house. It is a modern burial place, with a Catholic section, not one of the dear old-fashioned kind. The bronze plaque reads simply: "Anne Mary Geissler, January 29, 1958—March 27, 1959." Who would have thought it? Yet, it could happen to anyone or again to us.

Some neighbors and ourselves have bought graves in a group, so that there we shall also be buried. I know where I shall lie. It begins to be a little like another home—since we have no permanent home here—and another community where someone already is waiting for us. The cross and crucifix which the cemetery allowed us marks the spot. It also marks our faith in the resurrection on the last day.

As for mother, she is expecting still another baby, her fourteenth. There are those who would say it is one too many. Somebody who has lost a child knows it both ways—a child is a child is a child is a child. . . .

9
Postscript:
Seven Years Later

P ERHAPS this story has no ending. I put aside the postscript I wrote four years ago, and now it is, unbelievably, seven years since Annie died. Unbelievably too, in the last four years since writing it two new babies have been born to us. The one that was expected turned out to be Maura Judith, and the one after her, Mark Joseph. The oldest has entered the convent—all through Annie's intercession, Mother says. In fact, she took "Sister Anne" for her name "in religion." Few of us are as well perpetuated as that. As for mother she is expecting still another baby—at the end of the month. (Justin as it turned out.)

In those seven years since Annie died, the world has changed considerably, as everybody knows. I sometimes think that Annie and what she stands for is getting lost in all the preoccupations with the new world, though we ourselves who pray to her every day know better. What I mean is that a child is a child for its own sake, and in its own right. It continues to be the most defenseless and the most helpless of creatures, and in this new world seems to have fewer and fewer friends to speak for its abiding value.

When I think of these things, then Annie becomes a symbol of redemption, and her innocence draws out of me the kind of strength with which the weak are able to confound the strong. And mother and I, with our large family out of another world, continue to search for our place in the divine plan. And so it must be, as I keep faith with God the Creator throughout the day and into the night.

10
Postscript:
Nine Years Later

YESTERDAY evening during the children's hour—"when the night was beginning to lower"—my blonde little son and I went for a walk together, just himself and I. All the others were watching TV, but the two of us were left over—he, because he was too young for the show, and I, because I was too old. We wandered off to where our paths crossed in the kitchen.

. . . Lucky for us to meet that way, from the opposite ends of the earth. A child more than anything else that earth can offer to man . . . brings hope with it—and joy . . .

He looked up at me from down around my knees —every father is a big man to his little son—and I looked down at him from up around my six feet high. It is preposterous, ridiculous, unfair, that there should be such inequality between us whom need had just now made one. In a humble moment free of guile, he reached up as I reached down. A tremor of glee passed through his little body as we swung around cheek to cheek, neither one taller or shorter than the other now, and the father at least as happy as the son; the boy full of the joy of the man, and the man of the boy.

. . . It was not always this way. A father has to bide his time with babies. The first identity is with the mother—with softness, epitomized in the nursing breast, soft voice, soft flesh, soft hands, soft face, soft ways befitting to a little one. This first identity sometimes lasts surprisingly long—a year or even a year and a half sometimes . . .

The full-full moments of life are always short ones. It is something to know when they end, and a child can know it. At his command, I put down my little son and it might have ended there, a minute's experience in the long chain of growing up, but the little boy had other plans. He quick-legged it to the back door and when I didn't follow after, he came back after me. He took me by the hand and led me out, tall father and short son going for a walk in the cool warm of a September evening. The boy's idea really, but the man caught on now to what was happening, really happening, a happy happening to be handled gently with the gentle freedom of a new love.

. . . It is good for a child to begin to identify early with his father, but a father has to take it easy. The gruff voice, the pillowless, cushionless frame, the rough face, and the here-again, gone-again of the father are obstacles for a child to overcome. The identifying does not come all at once, but not so slowly either once it comes. It is easy to recognize the first big strides toward the father . . .

Outside I gave the boy his will with me, which was exactly what he wanted. I would be his foil, his sounding board, his high-strung instrument. No! I would simply be his father, the one he had led out the back door to make love with. He let go my hand and ran ahead of me twenty feet. He looked around and might have said: "Why aren't you running too?" I ran past him twenty feet, and when I looked around at him he laughed his little head right into the sky. Then at the sight of my crouching down he ran against me so hard that we both rolled over into the grass. Half a century apart, the two of us were rolling gleefully together in the grass.

. . . It is much easier for a little child to know his

father is playing with him than for a father to know when his child is ready to play with him most anytime. But it is a matter more of experience than of repetition. A child will remember that his father rolled with him in the grass. On the same level together, the identity comes easy. And a child remembers . . .

The dog came up to us now, big lumbering dog, and began to lick my face. Enough for me, but my little son did not mind so much and threw his arms around the neck of the big dog. The acceptance transformed the dog into a pillar of devotion, and I had to walk on alone while the two of them leaned against each other in mutual affection. I had to be satisfied for the moment with myself. They followed after me along the garden rows, and when I disappeared among the corn to pluck an ear, the boy was calling me. I gave him the ear, field corn with big kernels. He rolled it around and around in his hand. He squeezed it. He put it to his teeth, too hard to eat, but the sun shining on it made his nose look yellow.

. . . A little child, when first learning about the world, takes hold of things tenderly. He always expects the best at first. Some respond to him kindly, like the dog, and others, like hard corn, let themselves be done to as he wishes. But he doesn't like to be rushed with it, and a father must learn to take his time. If he does, a little child can teach a father how to be interested in everything. . . .

When we came to where the cow was on the other side of the fence, I asked the boy for the ear of corn, which he gave to me. I broke it in two for the cow and we watched the cow chew it heavily until it was gone. We saw it go down the long throat by the way it raised the skin on the cow's neck. The boy looked at me and then at the big cow tongue slobbering around for more. We were a long time there in front of the fence before the cow. We weren't scared at all. In the backyard again where we first tumbled in the grass, the boy let go my hand and went about picking up this and that and looking at it: a broken croquet ball, the shining silver of a discarded gum wrapper, a long-lost weatherbeaten clothes pin, an old bone.

. . . It takes a long time to get across a big yard with a little boy on a September evening. But it is better to go a hundred feet with him at his pace than a thousand other . . .

Little boy and I then fell into a game of hide and seek. I hid behind a tree too small to hide behind. I skipped to another which was bigger and only one side of me showed. I was losing the game. I went to the biggest tree and let him chase me round till he caught me by the knees and squeezed me.

Oh, the laughter of a little son delighting in his father's presence! It is like honey and the honey-comb. No wonder I sing a song of my little son Justin, eighteen-month old fourth son and sixteenth child, baby boy and best one yet—as mother has said of every one.

. . . Except Annie perhaps . . .

Part III

11
Art and Life Are Where You Find Them

I AM scarcely old enough to write my autobiography, and though I may someday be old enough to do so, I doubt that I shall ever be important enough to want to, or for it to matter whether I do or not. And yet I have come to believe that everyone has something to say. It's like my daughter Sarah said—and she only sixteen when she said it—"Everyone is an artist underneath." Art and life are where you find them.

I like to think that I have taught my children many things, and now I discover that the greatest teachers in my own life have been my children. Before they came I talked, when I did, in platitudes handed down to me from generations gone before, or handed over to me by the spokesmen of my own generation, by teachers of the grand traditions, by elders full of maxims, by newspaper heroes and their slogans, yes, even by books and schools. But almost the only things that have lasted and stood the test of time are the things I have come to know by my own efforts, by personal, intimate contact with earth and work, with flesh and blood people, by meeting the demands of human needs, and the final opening up to suffering, to others, and to a whole world always struggling.

But to achieve this you can't be forever a clod. You have to find the artist underneath. My daughter Sarah is further right: You have to go after this artist in you; you have to draw him out, give him birth, feed him, nurture him along, make something out of him, shape him and accept him as part of you, and open yourself to him as to your better half.

For life is not contained in platitudes, traditions, maxims, slogans and books. It is in you and me and other people, one at a time; and in the experience of grass and rain and wind, one at a time; and sweat and tears, pain and ache as experienced by you and me, one at a time; and in suffering, love, and friendship that open up in us the need to give and to receive. And neither is art something boxed and bound and banded, but something that suffers and shapes the self and communicates a firsthand experience of real life reality and receives another in return.

That I should by fifty have been dealt a new lease on life by the discovery of the art-reality of life is due not so much to the world of art coming into a new day, or even by explosion of color and form in this ongoing revolution of the last ten years, resulting in art all around us, but to the education of the father by his children. And this education, though iceberg-hidden in the exercise and the growth of free spirits around me, manifests itself simply in the childlike and guileless exposure of the hidden reality in the outward expressions of glee and joy, pain and sorrow, hope and fears, hunger and thirst, trust and confidence—all revealing the struggle and tensions of being and becoming, which are a child.

It seems to me, however, that two things are necessary for this education. First of all, you can't be forever a clod, as Sarah said, and being a father should help the normal person considerably in getting over this not so natural but very environmental handicap. Most of us have not been brought up as free spirits; we were born free and then weaned on the bottles of conformity and stereotype. It's like Rousseau said: "Man is born free but everywhere he is in chains." It almost takes the new vision of fatherhood to make us really see for the first time, to open our eyes to the art-reality of life, to educate us, if we are lucky, to art and life.

Even this isn't easy, for it is a matter of really seeing and really loving. Though it helps, being a father does not guarantee it either, but I think that in the long process of growing up, somewhere along the line a father will see—though he has looked at a thousand before—really see a child for the first time. Somewhere along the line, too, real loving will be required of him, and if he is up to it, his education by his children will have begun. Then he begins to see the art-reality in the world: the glee with which a child jumps because a ball bounces; the delight of rolling in the grass and the grace that is in it; the sensitive thrill in the fur of a kitten and the quivering urge to possess it; the pain in a rebuff from one on whom life depends, and the loneliness of waiting for the restoration of confidence ... and later on the tension of catching up with his father in his becoming, and the true anxiety in setting up his independence, and then even going beyond his father. ...

The other thing necessary for this education is the willingness to learn from everything and everybody, the openness to new things. Real growth in art and life comes to us from the outside as well as from within, comes to us from our relationships with other things and other people. It does not come to us from within or from without, but from within and without at the same time, so that we must always be building bridges. Without bridges we go nowhere. It is the genius of children in this matter that they know how to go out to other things and people, that they know how to build a bridge spontaneously and to establish a relationship easily.

Is it necessary that somewhere along the line this awareness and openness become submerged and obfuscated? Is it really a mark of adulthood to have overcome these "things of a child" and put on an armor of reserve and self-sufficiency? What happens to free spirits when they are reined in by the letters of laws and the circumscriptions of conventions?

I must admit that laws and conventions are necessary for orderly living, but the family's duty perhaps more than anybody else's is to develop free and open spirits, and not to repress and close off, but to open up and to expose, to make receptive and vulnerable to art and life. This has something to do with instilling the belief that everyone has something to say, that everyone is an artist underneath, that there is a better half to you and to me that needs to be kept alive.

12
Number One in
One Man's Family

"KITTY" was our first child and there was always this thing special about her that she was born shortly after I was sent overseas during World War II and by the time I saw her she was almost three years old. It seems we have always called her Kitty, though I recall a short period when she would have preferred to be called Kathleen, her real name.

There are other things, too, about Kitty that while not exactly special are the more vividly remembered because she was our first child. I don't know that anyone ever wanted a child more than we did when first we were married. Actually, we could hardly have had one more quickly as it turned out, but it worried us right from the start that the miracle might not happen to us. It didn't help either that my oldest and much revered brother, to whom I must have confided my worry, had said: "Oh, the babies! Oh, they will come quickly enough." They have indeed, but I just didn't believe that it would happen to us.

So with all the symptoms that today are so well recognized by us, we went to a doctor and he said that my wife was going to have a baby. I shall never forget how we looked at each other and how all the rest of the world became sheer unreality. The doctor had, in fact, to overtake us down the corridor to ask our name and where to send the bill. We had completely forgotten about him.

Then my wife and I were separated for a couple of months by my induction into the army. When she came to join me at the base, August 15, 1942, she was all beauty, radiance and delight . . . and bursting with wanting to tell me that "the baby moved yesterday." Perhaps, it would move again and I could feel it, she said. Well, of course, it did move again, and neither war, nor the seven seas, nor even second childhood will ever take that away from my remembering.

And then the first sight of her after the war.

I finally came back after thirty-four months overseas and was mustered out. I had the clothes on my back and my blue denim barracks bag, original issue, which had been with me half around the world—and that was all. For a while we sat together, the two of us—my bag and I—on the train going home at last, and I was surprised that I should be worrying about so grand a thing as coming home to my wife and child. After a while we made room for an older man in our seat, and I began to tell this man how it was inside of me coming home after so long a time away. But I didn't reach him, as they say now, and he preferred his paper to my little problems. It could have been he never was overseas, or even a soldier, and then it would be easy for him not to be interested.

There was a taxi strike in the little town and my wife met me on foot down by the tracks, and we walked the dozen blocks home. I was glad to get my bearings, one thing at a time. When we turned the corner off High Street onto Twelfth Street we were only two blocks away. This was my wife's town and there was a little delicatessen where we had picked up ice cream for her family four years ago when we first met.

Then we turned off Twelfth Street onto McCarty Street and now it was only a block. Then a half a block . . . and looking ahead I saw this fair-haired little girl leaning around the doorpost of the porch, peering down the street. Was she mine? Was that the house? She stepped out on the first step and waited. Everything about her was fair—her hair and skin and dress were all fresh and feminine fair. At the bottom of the steps I put out my arms to her. It was presumptuous of me. What more natural thing for a father to do? Though she might have done any number of other things, she came to me. This, too, I will always remember.

This is the little girl I think of tonight, wondering what her decision will be. She is 22 years old now. God has endowed her well, will he endow her some more? We have been blessed in her and will we be blessed again?

She was a bright child from the beginning. She won a scholarship to high school, edited the yearbook, and graduated with honors. She began college on two scholarships and took freshmen honors. I had it from others that she was a popular girl there.

With everything going her way, she did what in high school she had said she would never do. The Wednesday after Easter she called home to say that she had decided to enter the convent. I had gone to the National Catholic Education Convention in Detroit and wasn't home. When I did come home my wife was radiant . . . and bursting with something to tell me as she had been, now so long ago, when her first baby first moved in her womb. This was movement of life of a different kind but nonetheless real. This touch of the finger of God on us nothing shall ever take away from my remembering either.

We had a most satisfactory summer together that year, waiting for Kitty to enter in September. She came back from that year at college, matured, self-assured, thoughtful, generous. The grocery bill was up a bit with the new dishes and combinations she took upon herself, but the family was happy with the new variety. On her last fling at home, she was pleasing us all.

It is three years now since my wife and I took her and left her there at the convent—those parlors with all their correctness and the novice mistress knowing far better than ourselves how that "handing over" of her would come back to us again and again.

I got to thinking of her in the first place tonight because she is now in retreat in preparation for her taking of first vows. She has always been very happy when we visited her, but the last time, nevertheless, we became aware of the silent questions that put themselves forward perhaps only in the middle of the night and are answered only in the soul's solitude. They may be the same old questions every Christian must face, but I think they ask themselves more poignantly, more personally, in the convent, and are more complex in this mixed-up age than they have a right to be. This I know, too, that the questions never go away entirely—neither in my life, nor even after vows in hers, if it comes to that.

13
Number Two,
Age Nineteen

I HAVE always been fascinated by the answer of the eastern sage who, when asked for a sentence that would fit all times and occasions, remarked: "This too shall pass away."

As a sort of parallel to it, I have often asked myself the question: "How shall things be ten years from now?" In answer I have tried to imagine a flash of time in the future, just the glimpse of a moment ahead. On going to the war overseas, I wondered if I would even be there in that flash of a moment, what would my wife be doing, how many children would there be? Most often I would see a pleasant living room scene with mother and father and children around. If I projected the time forward during some crisis, the crisis was always dissipated by then. If I thought to do it during some time of great joy, the projection would only enhance it. Having poor capacity to imagine the worst, I always found the future encouraging.

The game, if it can be called that, goes a long way toward developing a positive attitude toward one's children. It helps to keep the present in balance with the future, the young girl with the woman, and the boy with the man. It is able to jump over adolescence in a given instance, long enough to adjust one's aim and equilibrium. It is able to relax one about the tempers of little girls and the foolish activities of little boys. It can sharpen expectations, nurture sanity, and even help shape the future by giving it a vision.

Mary, our second oldest, is now nineteen. I first wrote a little something about her ten years ago when she was nine. In it I wondered what would become of a little girl who acted so brashly in favor of other people. I called her "unalterably sympathetic." Her sympathy made a lot of problems for her even then, and I wondered how it would all come out with a person who acted so little from reason and so spontaneously from feeling. It was during one of these problems that I said to her in a burst of confidence: "I expect great things of you, Mary." The two of us have never forgotten this look into the future together.

How do I know that she has never forgotten it? Because in one way or another she keeps reminding me of it. In the eighth grade she won the grand prize in the Serra essay contest on the subject: "What I Would Do For God If I Had a Religious Vocation." I had not gone to the banquet that announced the winners, though Mother had. On returning home, Mary confronted me at the front door with this grand plastic prize as she said, "You always said you expected great things of me. Well, here it is." She was exceedingly gratified with herself to have lived up to expectations. So was I.

Her sympathetic directness toward other people's problems followed her into high school, into YCS, into other people's business (even into suggesting how the school should be run). She was as much in difficulty as she was out, it seems to me now, and when things were bad, as well as when they were worse, I would say to her again: "I expect great things of you, Mary." She ended strong, among the top of her class. As a senior she edited the yearbook, received the medal for art and art appreciation, and belatedly was inducted into the Honor Society. On the way up I heard another girl remark, "She couldn't care less." Just what that meant I didn't know, but Mary and I laughed together about all these great things happening to such an unlikely person.

At present, Mary is working her way through college on a staff scholarship, having somehow learned to be in on everything in spite of twenty-eight hours of staff work a week: YCS, the Cursillo movement, making her own clothes, babysitting for married students and profs, going to games and parties, achieving good grades—and being as always "unalterably sympathetic."

The other day I thought I knew that Mary had arrived, and I think I stopped worrying about how she was going to turn out. Nineteen is still young for a boy, but a girl is often quite mature by then. She has a philosophy of life now and is able to put her longtime feelings of sympathy into a framework. She acts now from reason as well as from feeling. I was one of the proudest fathers ever when I discovered it just lately, and I wish I could have imagined the scene ten years ago.

It happened on our trip to Wisconsin, the native land of the father of the family. It happened during a mild and easy after-dinner exchange between Mary and one of the adults.

In a way, the twentieth century has hardly arrived in some parts of the world, and both the secular and religious problems of our day are dealt with rather summarily—civil rights, ecumenism, human progress, war and peace. We adults like law and order. . . . Everything might somehow be settled by authority and obedience, by force and submission, by old days and old ways . . .

Mary began to take exception, or better perhaps, she began to spell out her philosophy: "But you can't treat other people that way. They are as good as you are. In fact, in the measure that you violate the integrity of another, you violate yourself."

"Now, you know, Mary, that every job has to have a boss and that it is a poor job that doesn't have a boss. There are those who have it and those who don't."

"I don't know about that. I only know that you need the other as much as the other needs you. There is a unique relationship, between every one and others which can't be duplicated by any other combination. For example, you are somebody to me nobody else is; you complement my personality in a way nobody else does."

"You mean that I have to fall over everybody that comes along? It adds up to a lot of confusion for me."

"The right attitude is essential. You are only somebody as you relate to others. You remain nothing if you keep a line between yourself and others. The relation of person to person which is now changing the world does not allow thinking in some of the old terms."

"But, Mary, there are those who amount to something because they help themselves and those who don't amount to anything because they don't care to help themselves."

"We have to respect everybody. Everybody, everything, has a truth, a beauty, and a goodness unique to itself, and I have to remain open to it. This is what you have to look for in people and things—including yourself. You can only recognize the good in others you see in yourself; you reject yourself insofar as you reject the good in others."

"You still have a lot to learn, Mary."

"That's just what I am saying. We all have—a lot to learn and a lot to grow. And we do it together. There is myself and others, and I identify only in relation with others. More than that. God himself is a community, and there is no being perfect like him without loving the other—whoever, wherever, whenever, however, we meet him. In the end we go to God together . . ."

14
...There Was a Wedding...

THERE was a wedding, first of all, in the garden of Paradise. It was the crowning point of creation. Through six long "days" God had worked up to it, prepared for it, taken great pains with it. Finally, he gave man and woman to each other and human love was born. God saw what he had done was *very* good, and he rejoiced within himself at what he had wrought. He blessed the man and woman and rested from his labors . . .

I have always thought that weddings should come off more simply than they do, and here were these two young people, Mary and John, age twenty and twenty-two, quite ready and satisfied to have a "simple liturgical wedding." But a simple wedding is not easy to pull off. For one thing, a wedding besides being a liturgical affair is immediately also a social affair. It is not only a sacrament, but also a celebration. It is an event that calls for rejoicing with friends as well as an exchange of vows in the presence of the Church and the community.

. . . Then there was another wedding, many years later, during the "eighth day of creation," in Cana of Galilee. The mother of Jesus was there, and Jesus also was invited, together with his disciples, to the wedding. Again there was rejoicing and again there was a blessing. Jesus, anticipating marriage with his own bride, renewed married love with a miracle. Henceforth there would always be sufficient "wine" for the Christian celebration of married love . . .

So there you are. From time immemorial there has been this religious and this social side to a wedding, and whatever else may be nonessential, the service and the feasting are not. The first real question was how to combine the service and the feast in the simplest way possible without losing any of the good things that make a wedding a happy and holy event, a worshiping and a rejoicing time. With this as our yardstick we got heads together with the young couple and our neighbors and discovered a surprising unanimity concerning what would go and what would stay. The burden of the big dinner would have to go, we said; rice, flowers, featured attendants, the wedding march, cameras and popping flash bulbs in church, would have to go. Hymns and songs, wine and friends, would have to stay.

. . . And then there is always a third wedding, when there is a wedding, and that is the wedding of this couple. Every wedding is always three weddings, and that is why a wedding is always a big thing . . .

Our basic decision was that the service and the feast would be one thing, and that the feast would follow immediately upon the service, that the liturgy would anticipate the social celebration immediately following it. We called this "the integrity of the celebration." For both aspects of this celebration we counted heavily on the help and presence of friends, neighbors, and members of the parish. What's a celebration anyhow—liturgical and/or social—without a community of people? We petitioned for an evening wedding Mass after dinner, and we would go from the nuptial Mass upstairs to the hall downstairs in the spirit of a liturgical-social celebration linked together as one.

. . . No wonder a wedding is such a grand affair. It is grand in its meaning and grand in its context, with a history back to the very beginnings of human life.

It really cannot be overdone except that it can become buried in its own embellishments . . .

The bride wore a chapel veil and a red and white suit made by her mother which she will no doubt wear again and again. Instead of flowers, the bride carried a special lighted candle decorated in sign and symbol which she will no doubt light again on special occasions long after the flowers would be gone. Instead of featured attendants, along with the staid and studied wedding march (the father never did give the bride away), the two families, the parents, the two official witnesses and the bride and groom joined the priest in the entrance procession to the altar, while the congregation sang Psalm 93: "Cry Out With Joy to the Lord!" This psalm has a long history, since Old Testament times, as a processional hymn. Only the bride and groom entered the sanctuary with the priest, the official witnesses staying in the pews with the families. The groom took the candle from the bride and put it on the Easter candlestick so that it might shine before all that were in the house.

. . . Every wedding is unique, and every wedding is a public sign of something new that has never been before. But in marriage this uniqueness is not something that isolates or withdraws, that hides or is hidden. The uniqueness exposes, proclaims, draws the light, diffuses its own gift—like a candle. Because every man is different, he is called upon to do his own thing. Because two differences are joined in marriage, uniqueness is enriched and multiplied, and the possibilities are those of the greatest adventure known to man . . .

The marriage ceremony, now in English, needed only to be enunciated clearly by the priest, which it was, to be impressive and appreciated. The many blessings are their own sermon now that they can be understood by the people.

At the Offertory the two official witnesses brought up the gifts of bread and wine. The bride and groom accepted them at the sanctuary and brought them to the priest. The congregation sang: "O Love That Nothing Can Efface."

The great Amen after the Canon really was the great Amen. If it is really to be the great Amen, it has to be sung several times over. It just cannot be the great Amen said or sung just once.

At Communion the wedding couple partook of the same bread and drank wine out of the same cup. The congregation sang: "God Is Love."

For the processional after Mass everybody sang "Now Thank We All Our God"; there are special verses for weddings.

. . . The wedding couple is at the dawn, not only of a new thing and a new day, but also at the dawn of original creation and its renewal. Everything is theirs for the having. No wonder that we rejoice. No wonder that we sing. No wonder that we wonder what the new day, the new dawn, the new creation and the new renewal will bring . . .

Downstairs, wines and cheeses, breads and cookies were available on tables immediately beyond the receiving line.

We had as much as possible discouraged gifts—though not too successfully as it turned out. What we wanted instead was the people themselves to rejoice with us, and if they wanted to bring something, a contribution of wine or cheese, bread or cookies, was welcome. For once, people said, they felt like part of the wedding.

The wedding cake was extraordinary, provided by a friend of the family and a friend of Mary's. So the celebration downstairs worked up to that with a special drink for all and a toast by the father of the bride. He toasted all friends present, he toasted the newly married couple on the threshold of so great an adventure as the founding of a family, and he toasted God and the groom's parents for having provided so fine a son.

. . . We stand beside each other, my wife and I, at this wedding of our daughter, recalling our own, interpreting every possibility in terms of the success and failure of our own: the warm light of fresh morning, the fierce noonday heat of long commitment, and the foretaste now and then of walking in the garden with God in the cool of the evening . . .

Because the weather featured one of the worst snowstorms of the century, only half the guests were able to make it. It is hard to postpone a wedding.

. . . This marriage is theirs now and we are hardly more than spectators. Do they look at us as we look at them? Will they remember us as we remember them? Will they draw strength from us, understanding, when they need it? Will they go beyond us in love? What they see in us is something that came later: a fire subdued, a candle burning low, a quiet passion of little signs that do not impress the young. We were overwhelmingly in love on our wedding day. Maybe they are too and maybe their love will be sufficient for them, as ours has been for us . . .

It was a good wedding as I remember it, all things working together for good: hymns and psalms, vows and blessings, Mass and Communion; best wishes and wine; songs, talk and laughter—and the beginning of a new Christian family. A lot like other weddings, only a little different.

. . . We didn't know, and they don't know, what it all means to marry and to be married. In fact, the weddings in which we are most involved are also those in which we are most preoccupied with externals. This is always distracting. It comes clear only later what it means, really means, to be married to this man and to this woman, or for the daughter to be married to this son. But this I do know: God saw what *he* had done and it was *very* good.

15
Number Three,
Age Eighteen

IF EVER I developed great expectations for any-body in the family, I developed them for Sarah, now eighteen. For the present, however, I am wait-ing. What I am waiting for is not easy to define.

For five, for ten, for fifteen, sixteen, seventeen years you do for your child according to your lights. You are able to do a lot. Then, rather suddenly, you can't do much anymore. Instead, you wait; the ini-tiative isn't yours anymore.

Sarah is in a special way our creative one, just how creative I didn't know for a long time. For many years her creativeness did not take on, as I re-call now, any definite form. Yet, she could entertain the younger part of the family for hours with a few pieces of string and a few ends of paper. Whatever was at hand, indoors and out, lent itself under her sure touch to a thousand improvisations. She would see a hundred combinations where I might see one. She didn't talk much (she still doesn't), but what she said, and above all what she did, always had a good audience—and a long line of imitators. Part of her secret was that she managed to make her crea-tiveness contagious, and it has had its response, immediate and far ranging, in many members of the family. Truly, things are different in our world be-cause of Sarah.

So, while Sarah was in the upper grades we might have a skit or play most any Sunday afternoon, or a puppet show or a party with ingenious and outland-ish decorations, and if you didn't have imagination yourself, you would hardly know what was going on. The little children with their lively imaginations always loved it; they knew a dream world when they saw one.

It was at this time, too, that she started to haunt the place, as I have come to call it. Every nook and cranny and corner of our outdoors have come to know Sarah and Sarah has come to know them—intimately. We do have some acres; they zigzag from the road, 500 feet in front of our house, to an osage orange hedge in back of our house, for a total of almost half a mile. These acres Sarah has roamed and combed, turned over and kicked around, squeezed like an orange and worried like a dog does a bone, through all the sweet years of her young life, to make them yield their secrets. She has brought in stones and bones and animal teeth, branches of thorn and clumps of weeds and insect carcasses . . .

We would find these things in her room, which though not very well kept was always an interesting room. Or we might find them in the long basement room under the kitchen, which came in time to be known as "Sarah's art room." We would find them in one of those hundred combinations of things where I might see only one. Altogether, Sarah herself and Sarah's bedroom and Sarah's art room have been a disorderly but creative influence in our house. I have come to sense by a kind of osmosis from being around Sarah that for young people, at least, too much order and orderliness is not conducive to the creative spirit. "Order is heaven's first law," and "Cleanliness is next to godliness," and perhaps too "The good child is an obedient child," turn out in the end to be just half truths. Other things are, at any rate, more important in drawing out the human spirit.

At the age of thirteen, Sarah made a discovery. She discovered colors along with her combinations. And she discovered that she could draw, paint, carve and do mosaics and crude sculpture; she discovered the file and the chisel, the line and the curve. Almost immediately she won the art prize in high school as a freshman, and again as a junior. Always most outstanding was her sense of color and her sense of composition; her sure eye for how things go together, not so much in nature—certainly her first teacher—but how things go together in the hands of a new creator, in new combinations and colors, on paper, in crayon, in pastoil, in collage; in wood, in enamel, in cloth. . . .

During the three or four years, from about thirteen to sixteen, she was extremely generous with her special talent. We would never know what she would come up with next. My wife and I would always be pleasantly surprised at Christmas by another creation of Sarah's—a mosaic of a pelican and her young, a Byzantine Madonna, a wood carving of a tall mother and child, a wire and glass "house of God," and for two years running she designed a "Christmas Holy Family" and an "Epiphany Holy Family" which I was able to manufacture out of wood into Christmas gifts of our own.

On certain birthdays she literally made storybooks for the children—completely her own creations from text and illustrations to sewing and binding. *Why Frogs Go Glug-Glug* will undoubtedly go down in the family lore for generations, and *Gluggeger,* the dog boy, tired of caring for "Molindie, Gdoz, Timox and the queen dog, Razdaz," will be remembered long after more important things have been forgotten.

At school she did a whole string of posters, cards, programs and arrangements...

And then, almost as suddenly as it began, it all seemed to grind to a halt—not so suddenly perhaps, except that one day I realized Sarah was not producing in the same way anymore.

It is about a year now and that is why I am waiting. It is a father's wait for his child to find herself and again come to life.

As I wait, I wonder why I have never been able to establish better communication with Sarah, and why the little there was seems to be less. I rationalize to myself that that is the way artists are and that is the way artists must be—with a carefully guarded inside world of their own where they keep their own counsel. It must be so, because I always have the feeling when I see Sarah on one of her lonely walks or bareback on the horse against the hedge, that she is not lonely at all but communing with herself, in her own world.

As I wait, I worry how her future seems to hang on small threads, how so much depends on her finding herself, and even on what just happens to happen to her right now. There is no way of hurrying her along and hardly any way of helping her, except on her own terms. Perhaps, it is her time to lie fallow, like a field, in order to bear much fruit later. I hope so.

What worries me most is that her special talent

might yet go wasted, that she may never discover the long and laborious distance between talent and artist. Wouldn't it be terrible, I say to myself, if she never came to the new life because of some little this or that, if the difference between success and failure is something that I did or did not do?

Alas and alack! Beside the river of life I sit with my expectations, waiting for the help of the Lord.

16
Number Four,
Age Seventeen

TEN YEARS ago I wrote something about Sheila that suggested she had difficulty in taking her turn in a conversation. There was always something at the end of her tongue that wanted saying immediately. Watching the counterplay with some of the older ones (she is fourth in the family), I had written that "Sheila is seven years old and always quick with an answer." Yes, even at seven she was rarely ever bested in a battle of small talk. Accused at the age of seven of being noisy in bed beyond curfew, she merely answered, "I was saying my rosary." The fact was, she just might have been saying her rosary, and it had to end there, for how can you come back at a little girl whose only fault was that she was saying her rosary?

That was ten years ago. Sheila is now seventeen, a senior in high school and still quick with an answer. The answers are perhaps a little more polished now —she is literary editor of the yearbook—but they are just as genuine as they were at seven: warm, mercurial, clever, generous, humorous—and abundant. And I like to think that they also still have that touch of the rosary about them—they are never meant to hurt anybody. Whether they are meant to do so or not, they merely make people laugh.

I am convinced that every family should have a Sheila, and that no family should give up until it does. A Sheila is worth waiting for. Though our Sheila is fourth in a long line—providence having probably provided her early to lighten our load—she would still be a gem if she were seventh, or ninth, or twelfth. . . . At any rate, a family does not know what it is missing until it has a Sheila.

And that is true of every child.

Right now, Sheila is at the dining room table slugging it out with the typewriter. Some of the yearbook copy is due. "Literary editor of the yearbook! Ha! An editor edits somebody else's stuff, doesn't he? I write it one night and then edit myself the next." She types a little more and then says, "Get going, Sheila. The joke's on you." The disposition is enviable. Sheila, incidentally, genuinely likes the sound of her own name and is able to talk about herself in the third person. I am reminded of the difference between wit and humor. The wit can make a big story—two weeks later—out of his falling out of the boat, but the humorous man can laugh at himself right then and there when it happens. That's Sheila.

I look down the long line of my children, and when I finally get to Sheila—tall, dark, handsome and gay—I wonder just exactly what God has in mind for her. Already at seventeen she has made her small world a better place to live in.

I must remember to dream some really big dreams for her.

Still, the essential Sheila is not the merely quick and funny one. It does accentuate her, and brings out the taste, as it were, but it is not the essential Sheila. The essential Sheila has a universal ring to her. Not everyone can be quick on the trigger and funny, but everyone can be himself—his true self.

When you think of her in this way, her name is legion. There are millions like her who don't pretend to be anybody but themselves. They are the truly good people that everybody else takes for granted, in the homes, in the schools, in the offices, wherever the wheels of life are turning. I do not mean that they are ordinary people, but lacking special or outstanding talents in this or that, they have just themselves to give.

Because she is a senior in high school, Sheila is getting catalogs from colleges now. She doesn't really know where she would like to go, or what she would like to study, or what she would like to be. "Shall I go to this women's college, or that small co-educational college where the men outnumber the women three to one, or a big state university? What do you think, Daddy?"

"Where you can get the most help," I say. I mean it, too.

But Sheila says, "Oh, be serious, Daddy."

"Maybe you ought to decide first what course you want to take, and what you want to do with your life."

"Well," she says in her frank way, "if you put it that way, I want to get married and have a family."

"In that case, go to that 'three to one' college."

That only settles it for a little while. "Look, this college wants to know what I want to major and minor in. I just have to decide, Daddy."

"OK, you are good in English, and you like history."

"I get along well in math. Maybe I ought to take some more math."

"Look, they have a major in theology. I think you ought to major in theology. Nothing is more interesting than theology."

120

"I think maybe I would like to get into psychology . . . and sociology."

All this has a kind of universal ring to it, too. It isn't exactly that Sheila, like so many others, can't make up her mind. I was going to say that it is because she is a jack of all trades, but that is not doing her justice. She is just good at a lot of things in a general way—the whole gamut of high school subjects, and with her hands at doing things: domestic things at home, clerical things in an office and good with children and people. There are a whole lot of these "general" persons and though they all vary in the degree of their general gift, together they are a great blessing on mankind.

Sheila has trouble making up her mind about where she wants to go to college, and what she wants to take, and what she wants to be, not because she is indecisive, but because the decision is a real one. The person with a specific talent knows what he is best at, but the person with the general ability really does have a number of alternatives to choose from.

A dash of irrepressible lightheartedness, an essential knack for being her balanced self, and a lot of general ability that makes it hard for her to decide just exactly how to confine and limit herself, that is Sheila's unique combination.

Lincoln once said that there was always teaching and politics to go into. Not being thick-skinned enough to be a politician, Sheila will probably end up being a teacher. That is a big dream for her: a good teacher, I have always said, is worth his weight in gold.

Part IV

17
A Time to Wonder Why

I HAVE in the previous section written briefly—and selectively—about some of my older children. It has been enlightening and soul-searching. Perhaps I have never thought so seriously about my children before; perhaps it was not even possible to take them so seriously before they had reached a certain age. In fact, rather than just talk about them and tell little stories about them, I discovered I was analyzing them instead, and that discovery scared me a little. To say the least, it made me wonder why. Also, it has made me wonder about life.

For many years I was editor of some family features. There was one curious thing I discovered rather early in this work. For every ten or twenty mothers or fathers who were willing to write about family life or children while their children were small, it was almost impossible to find one who would write about family life or children once their children had reached adolescence and were older.

At first, I ascribed some facile reasons for this, like the glamor of children having worn off by then, or even the glamor of writing having worn thin after so long; like life having gotten too busy with the cares of the world or the enthusiasm for it having waned. There is some truth in all of these, but the basic truth is not that the parents have gotten older, but that the children have. And the answer is not merely that some of the glamor is gone. If I didn't appreciate those few parents who have written about their older children before me, I do so now.

What happens to children as they grow up? They not only grow up but also away. The circle of life grows ever wider and wider. What is characteristic about "teenagers" (a term they do not like)? They are children who have in a way arrived, who have begun to jell. I like to think of them as adults, I like to treat them as equals, I like to leave a lot of decisions up to them. They don't really need me in the same old way anymore. In fact, I should not have called them "children"—or "teenagers" either. I was right in writing about them to call them by name.

That is not all. They are young adults, and they present some of the problems that always arise among adults who have to live together and associate rather closely and at length with each other. This is the problem of community life—less the problem of obedience and authority than the problem of freedom and order. Freedom and order— what a combination! It is the time for a father to discover the meaning of latitude and elasticity.

But what is it, really, that scares a father to write

about teenagers when he is so close to them? The first reason I think is that there is always a touch of wishful thinking about their maturity, and that part of the outcome during what is called adolescence is always in the balance: will they make it? Looking at the world through one's own eyes of experience, it doesn't seem possible that they ever can. It is a good thing that they do not have the eyes of experience, that way they can be more single-minded about their ideals and ambitions.

At any rate, it is no time to be writing about them, or to be analyzing them. Looking at the bright side, it is like going out on a limb, to be a pollyanna perhaps; looking on the dark side is not only unpleasant but probably unfair, a lack of faith perhaps. There is no way of winning.

In the second place, they are becoming somebody else, really somebody else, and it is not so easy to know them anymore. There is more to them than there was at two, six, and twelve years of age when they were hardly more than an extension of home and parents. In fact, there is so much to them now that they are becoming complicated and complex. All the forces of their lives, and they are many—physical, social, psychological, emotional—are shaping up into a new personal combination quite distinct from any other. Not everything is under control anymore; they have slipped away into not just anybody else, but somebody else—into something both subjective and objective, an individual and a person.

On account of the new complexity it isn't enough just to tell a story about them anymore. There is more to them than that. There is so much to them in fact that when you are finished you are not even sure of your analysis. You may not even be sure of yourself anymore, to what extent you have been doing the right thing all along. It is only parents of the young who have all answers.

Last of all and most important, life with one's own teenagers requires a reexamination of old values, or as the saying goes today, a reevaluation. It is necessary to face life again, brought to the judgment seat through the eyes of one's own children. It seems to me now that there are three times in the normal course of life when it is necessary to face up to life: during one's own adolescence, then during the adolescence of one's children, and lastly I suppose toward the end of life in the face of death. I know that some people never face up to real life values because they aren't that serious about life, but the opportunity—or the challenge—does come at the time of one's own adolescence. It is no small matter either, sometimes taking as long as seven years (or more) to resolve. But when the matter is settled it looks like it is good for a lifetime.

It isn't. Life values come up for challenge and a new opportunity again a whole generation later. I mean there is a real personal encounter with life values a second time—just as real as and just as personal as the first time with all its turmoil, jostling and readjustment.

Not all this is painful, and none of it needs to be dull, but it is necessary to learn to listen—not always easy for a father. The new outlook on life and its values, especially in this day of change, needs to be in terms of a give and take, a sharing of experience. While it is all going on during the "second adolescence," as during the first, the strong tendency is to play it close to the chest, just like a teenager. (I shall return to this whole point again in the last chapter.)

18
Number Five,
Age Sixteen

Molly is sixteen today (December 8), having been born by a special effort of her mother on the Blessed Mother's feastday, just before the day ran out. Because Molly skipped a year in grade school, she is now a junior.

It is a continuous surprise to me just how old Molly really is. When the experts say that "maturity is not a matter of years," I think of Molly. In the way it really counts, Molly has been mature for a long time. Her attitude toward life and her reactions to people and events are first of all her own and secondly well beyond her years. I think it is because she is a Christian. Different people encounter Christ at different times in their lives; you can almost spot the time if you are close enough. Molly encountered him early in life.

Molly's maturity and "Christianity" have built up in me a considerable respect for modern young people. She is not typical of some of them, but on the other hand she is representative of what most of them feel, I think. And as far as I am concerned she "redeems" them all by her utter sincerity and simplicity about what is important in life. For me teenagers can never be just difficult, tensed up, cantankerous, moody or rebellious anymore.

Molly is a rebel. There is no use kidding anybody either; to be a true rebel is not for weak characters, and nobody gets by just putting it on for a trimming, because the trimming will show all too quickly. The good rebel, the true rebel, is, like a prophet out of the Old Testament, not only sent by God, on fire with a touch of the divine, but a strong character to begin with, single-minded, unwavering, magnetic, with a strong sympathy for the lowly. The comparison on face value says too much when applied to Molly, but these are the things she makes me think about.

Just the other day Molly said to me: "Do you know who my closest friends are at school?"

"No, who?"

"The cleaning ladies," she answered; "they are so real." It didn't surprise me. Nor would it have surprised me if she had said the students or teachers or some particular part of them.

That same day downtown she chanced upon four Negro children of the same family, from the section where she had worked at the settlement house on Washington Street all summer. "Oh, Daddy!" she said, "I'm so lonesome for Washington Street!"

She gravitates toward "lost causes" and is always on the suffering side of the rich-poor, strong-weak, big-little confrontations in the world. "What people need," she will say, "is not money, but other people."

All this is fare for adults, and because Molly is "only sixteen" and still "just in high school," it can only mean so much in terms of action, and she is often frustrated. But I have come to believe that it is all very genuine with her, that her rebellion, mild as it is right now, against war and violence, against the commercializing of the human and overlaying of the holy in the world and in each one of us, against the weight of systems and structures, is authentic, and calls forth from her the prophetic, and if necessary, lonely witness of the gospel.

Again this is saying too much about Molly. These

are my words, not hers, but this is the vision I see. In her it is a seed springing up.

How important do I think it is to be a true rebel? Christ was one.

In a school that is geared to academics, and they all are these days, Molly is continually having troubles. She bumps against "the system," with its tyranny of grades and its batteries of tests, its conformity of person to structure, its intellectual bias. Sometimes I end up wondering, with Molly, if our whole educational structure needs a Pope John to open some windows. It would be easier for both of us if she just conformed, but I like to think that Molly is getting a better education in spite of it. She is getting one befitting Molly.

Systems and structures are always very complicated and complex, so of course it is never entirely fair to want to tear them down and get rid of them, the wheat with the chaff. I am ready to compromise, to beat Molly over the head about grades, and lay down the law to her. But Molly isn't ready to compromise; she has all the single-mindedness of the prophet. For the present she will do enough to get by, pay a token of respect to the system, and enlarge herself on her own terms. And because her own terms are so unassailable—the social-mindedness, the penchant for the poor and needy, the spirit of poverty, the Christian witness, the simplicity of the gospel, joy of life, respect for the human person . . . should I lend a finger toward crushing such a spirit?

Every person is exceptional. Molly too has her gifts; nature has been kind to her. But that is just the point. She has to find herself amid these gifts; she has to find herself in spite of these gifts; she has a right to become her own master so that she will use these gifts for the only thing that matters.

Among the influences in her life outside of home is certainly the school with its community of students, teachers, and working people—all of them persons to Molly, because it is persons that she values rather than classes, books, traditions and knowledge for its own sake. Among the influences too is Grailville, that feminine woman's place in Loveland, Ohio, where Molly has spent part of two summers; Dorothy Day's *The Catholic Worker* with its simple barebones gospel of brotherhood; St. Peter Claver House on Washington Street; the guitar, discovering her singing voice, and the 1001 folk songs; the playing and singing at friendship Masses; the contact with Friendship House; dramatics and parts in plays; winning a trophy for dramatic interpretation; art class and the experience of expression in shapes and colors. . . .

It all sounds like a peripheral merry-go-round, doesn't it? Yet it seems to me that it is in extracurriculars that Molly is finding herself, and the great discovery may well be that she can communicate, that she can reach others.

In the new Church and the new world that is breaking, the ability to reach others will be more important than many other things. Perhaps she can make a career out of that.

19
Number Six,
Age Fifteen

DURING the stages of growth it is a dramatic moment when a child walks for the first time. It is dramatic because he knows and his father knows when he has taken his first step, and both exult in the accomplishment. There is a time before and after; before he didn't, now he does. The talking, which may well be more of an accomplishment, is never so dramatic because who knows when a child has really said his first word? Like the Eskimo mother, asked if her little child talked yet, remarked: "Oh, he has been talking since he was born; we just don't know what he is saying." So many of the human accomplishments in life are much more like the talking than the walking. When did it really happen? The first six or seven years of life are especially full of one new accomplishment after another.

Nora, fifteen this month and sixth oldest in the family, made me aware of a child's effort during these years to push forward to the next accomplishment and to the next stage. If it didn't happen, she made it happen. Some children try harder to crawl, to walk, to talk, to play, to make things . . . and the effort pays off.

Then there comes a nice, quiet, peaceful period in a child's life which is a special boon to parents, roughly the second six or seven years—not really "quiet" but settled and without turmoil. But again, the entry into this period is not so definitive that one can say just when it happened. What is definite is that the child who has arrived at this point in his development fits in well with the family, wants to help, can be depended upon, and really has no big problems. (There are exceptions, of course, when something has gone wrong somewhere along the line and he never quite achieves this nice, quiet, peaceful period. That is sad.)

Nothing went wrong with Nora though I worried about her during this stage. Her reaching out beyond her years got her into many small troubles. In the middle of a large family a child has to stay in his place to get along. I worried about Nora's being "put in her place" so often by so many people. Mother said that I shouldn't worry about Nora. Nora will come out all right, she said. And Nora did. By the middle of this second period she had become one of the most capable, helpful, and resourceful persons in the house. By the time she finished grade school she was ready for high school: secure, self-confident, able and willing. Early in her freshman year, when the religion teacher said: "Well, if any of *you* want to try to teach the next class . . . ," Nora raised her hand. As it turned out, Nora took it seriously and prepared, but the teacher did not, and so it never came off. However, Nora was ready and willing.

I have come to believe that this golden period is crucial for adolescence, and that there is such a thing as being able to take adolescence in stride if a child has had a nice, quiet, peaceful second period. At least I hope so.

I have also come to believe that one of the most exciting things for a father is to watch the transition of his child from this nice, peaceful, quiet period into the next. It takes a little time to make the transition, as everybody knows, but what everybody doesn't know is that the transition can be quite delightful and satisfying—and even relatively short. What people call adolescence with a shudder and teenage with a touch of desperation may not and need not last that long at all, or be that difficult at all. The difficult part may come and go in a year, and the other five or six years of this third period be really quite satisfying.

So I expect it to be with Nora, now at the point of transition from girl to woman.

It is exciting for a father to watch his girl grow into womanhood, but it is not like a child taking his first step: yesterday, no; today, yes. Though there is a point before and after in the physical development of a girl, the physical development into a woman is nevertheless gradual. The psychological and social development even more so. Just when did any girl begin to act like a woman? It is hard to tell. What is a woman? One week there are some signs of it. Then there aren't any for a while. Then next week there are some more.

I heard a man on radio recently talking about how a girl becomes a woman overnight. I most certainly felt he was oversimplifying. Did he mean that because she menstruated for the first time she is a woman now, or she had a date, or she fell in love and suddenly she is a woman? Somewhere along the line this is part of the process, but growing into a woman, as everybody knows, is much more complex than that.

Nora's strong point, I think, is people—a sense of people, an interest in people, and a real delight in people. She is sociable, spontaneous, open—prerequisite qualities, and Nora has them. I used to think when she always wanted to be first to welcome a visitor to our house, it was in the interests of being the first one there—something like winning a race. But I have come to think now that it is a genuine fondness for people. Someone who has come often to our house, remarked to me one day that he can always expect a warm welcome from Nora. The welcome is even warmer now, as she does it with more dignity and indeed more depth. The quick smile and the laughing eyes and a real interest in the person never leave any doubt about it.

In regard to people she has always been, I think, interested in the whole cross section of them—not only her own age, but also older and younger ones. She can manage, too, a measure of communication with both sexes. She is not inhibited about asking people about themselves, and can start and carry on a conversation with a certain amount of ease and interest.

When I tried at one time to analyze the basic needs of teenagers, communication was certainly one, and the ability to carry on a conversation—communication at its most elementary—with a cross section of people seemed to me a necessary and worthwhile goal to work toward. Such a teenager is already a long way toward having a grasp of himself.

The corollary of being able to communicate is to have something to communicate. I have sometimes called Nora our storyteller, but it is a special kind of storytelling. It is not the kind that conjures up dragons, multiplies plots, and creates a whole new world —that is storytelling of a special kind. Nora's stories are real stories about real people. The panorama of human life as it unfolds before her every day is full of things to talk and tell about: little things and big things, joyful things and sad things—each human event or impression has a nugget of drama in it clustered about with little details. The story is never the quick aside of the wit when she tells it, nor even the warm joke of the humorist, but something about life that has a beginning, middle and an end. It is not told to make anyone laugh, though sometimes it does; it is a chunk of life, take or leave it.

There is a sense, I think, in which these two fine qualities—people-loving and storytelling—are in reach of everyone. Humanity calling forth a personal response of human sympathy, compassion and warmth looks above all to woman for an answer. My dream for Nora is the woman who answers yes to humanity through love and communication.

20
Number Seven,
Age Fourteen

THE FIRST BOY in the family was a revelation. We had not yearned for a boy like some people thought we were yearning having already six girls in a row. Girls are nice, as the saying goes, and for us they really were, and we were not saying it just as a consolation. Nor were we just having more girls in the hope of having a boy. We never had a penchant, or the need, for being that analytical about it anyway—nor the audacity perhaps to think of God in that way. Post-natal analysis of the ways of God would hardly have occurred to us who were so thoroughly satisfied and grateful for things the way they were. Not even the professional cadres of social change sent in "to rub raw the sores of discontent" could have found the necessary discontentment.

A long time later those six girls in a row are still . . . nice.

All this talk about six girls is by way of introduction to the first boy, number seven in the family. As I said, the first boy was a revelation. To an observant and sensitive mother, he was different from the very beginning. While he was yet untouched by culture to teach him ways different from the girls, he was already different. His mother knew when she nursed him—not just when she changed him—that this was so. There never was any doubt about the genetic potential of the boy being different right from the start.

There is a certain generosity about God revealed to us in various ways, and one mark of this generosity is the diversity among men, as among creation in general. One aspect of this generosity of God was revealed to us by the first boy against a backdrop of girls. There are things we hear all our life and they mean little to us because we have not experience of them. Or we have had some experience of them and see them obscurely, and then after further experience of them, in some new way, less obscurely.

It is there in Scripture, in a section so succinct that every word counts. And in this section where every word counts, the sacred writer has taken the trouble to make the distinction which everyone knows, but only more or less obscurely in the depths of its mystery. The obvious distinction is an important part of his story. For the mother and the father of the first boy mentioned earlier, the darkness is less and the light is more which surrounds the fundamental distinction of mankind into girl and boy: "In the image of God he made them. Male and female he created them."

Without reference to cultures and kingdoms, without reference to peoples and races, universal man is male and female. What does it mean? What will it yet mean? But a mother and father of girls and boys know that the difference is real and penetrating.

We called the first boy Peter and part of the revelation was that Peter didn't like to be contained, circumscribed, limited—even by his mother's arms—except when he was nursing maybe. The spirit of the boy was a restless and free spirit right from the start. The baby bed with the sides up was all right when he was fast asleep, but it was only a challenge before and after. He would shake it around the room at a surprisingly early age, if not because he wanted out, then surely because he wanted to see what he could do with the thing. It is symptomatic of how the physical world is regarded by the boy. If God gave both male and female the command to rule the world and dominate it, then the boy's approach was much more in the nature of a direct attack upon any part of it he could get his hands on. If he were ever to arrive at a formula for dominating the physical world indirectly through the spiritual, this was something that would come only later, if at all.

When Peter first faced the outside world, at the age of two, it was different again. It was a place right from the beginning to be explored and if possible taken apart and investigated that much more thoroughly. There was not too much regard for putting it back together again, much more a kind of endless, sometimes maddening, thirst to lay it open to scrutiny. As far as I can tell, a boy arrives only slowly, if at all, at an equally strong interest in synthesis to balance his propensity for analysis.

When Peter became a little older, and could ask questions and I could try and answer them, there were a great many questions and a great many answers. But the answers never did really satisfy the boy. They might do for a while but the boy had mostly to prove it for himself, to find out for himself, to test and when possible to know firsthand. It is one of the reasons, I think, that boys get there more slowly, arrive later at the real issues of what we generally call "life," and why there is perhaps a kind of perpetual adolescence about them hard to outgrow. They engage themselves for a long time on the physical periphery of life and seriously engage life itself only at certain particular moments of confrontation—with love, with the other, with suffering, with failure, with death.

Peter is now fourteen and can be counted on around the place to do a lot of things his father does or his father used to do. He has come a long way. The fact is we are in a kind of friendly competition in relation to the garden work, the barn work, the lawn work, the tractor work, the caretaking and repair work of our large-family institution. That so much of this work has been around has been a boon to the boy. The second boy will not have it so good. The boy and I complement each other nicely in ruling and dominating our little bit of physical universe. We experiment with it, we enlarge on it, we improve it, in a word we dress and keep the garden which the Lord has given us: he for the motive of doing it and finding out for himself, and I from the motive of serving life with it. He is on the periphery, like I said, and I, long since swamped by human considerations, fit it into my engagement with real life.

I look at Peter ready for high school now, on the eve of his final physical growth, and wonder when his real engagement with life will come, and what confrontation will be the cause of it when it does come. What touch of grace from the outside, what prompting of love from within, what discovery of "the other," what insight into the spirituality of life will turn his head toward the serious side of reality?

There is something steady and firm about this boy of fourteen, there is something invincible and self-made, something not to be pushed around about him, something free and uncommitted. There it is ... needing a piece of revelation of its own to give it purpose.

21
...Peter the Worker...

PETER and his father had first talked, as far back as last November, when the cow was brought in for the winter, how the fence around the cow pasture would have to be fixed next year or the cow would surely break out and chomp up the neighbor's garden.

Or, worse still, she would get into the neighbor's backyard and, like another cow ten years ago, eat another slip off the clothesline. That kind of thing rarely makes good neighbors.

Peter had grumbled about it: "Oh, that fence is all right, and I am not going to do all that work just for the helluvit."

Peter always reacted like that about a job to begin with. It was his way of being independent. He might as well have said: "You can't push me around, see; I'll do it if I want to and when I want to."

It sounds farfetched I suppose, that part of a boy's upbringing these days might be taking care of a cow, but for various reasons we have never been without a cow. Taking care of a cow is a real education for a boy.

There she is, well over half a ton, fairly safe and very reliable, generally cooperative and well meaning, but nevertheless imposing—and needing a lot of man-sized care, which if given produces tangible results for the common good, clearcut satisfaction, and even some maturity.

Consider how that half-ton of living reality must be met on her own terms, how she cannot be pushed around, how she cannot be forgotten about. If she doesn't have water, she will bellow; if a gate is left open she will get out; if her feed is neglected she

149

will drop in milk. Every day, winter and summer, rain or shine, morning and night, she is waiting. She will perk up, her ears forward and her head toward the boy, when he comes in to feed and milk her. To feed her seems easy in the summer—if the fence is good and the pasture is kept up; easy in the winter, too, if, according to the rhythm of the seasons, food for the winter was put away in the summer. To milk her seems easy (it really isn't), but to see a cow through the biological cycle from calf to calf—and five or six hundred milkings—well, it's not like reading a book about responsibility.

I wish every growing boy could have the chance of taking care of a cow for a year or two—or at least a paper route, if that is the modern substitute.

Peter at fourteen has been taking care of the cow since he was eight. I can still see that eight-year-old boy, six-thirty on any winter morning, going through the snow or wind or cold, without having been awakened or reminded about it. When he would sometimes complain and grumble, or even say, "that damn cow, anyhow," I never said much, taking my cue from the cow, who didn't either.

But the fence! Three months after we had first talked about the fence it was the middle of winter, and Peter asked about cutting down the row of dying locust trees "in the back." He wanted something to do for exercise, he said. There were about fifty of these trees, planted ten or twelve years ago to alternate with maples. They had trunks about ten inches thick, and the job of cutting them down and trimming them out kept Peter busy for about a month of winter spare time.

Then it was spring again, the grass green, and the cow out to pasture again. "Peter" I said, "we are going to have to take care of that fence."

"But, Daddy, I told you that fence is all right. If you want to do something with it, okay, but I am not."

"I'll get you a new roll of barbed wire and all you have to do is stretch it, nail it, and that will reinforce the whole fence. You don't even have to take the old one down."

That exchange was in April or May and nothing happened until the middle of June, when all of a sudden Peter was after it in earnest. He had the wagon behind the tractor and was loading posts (the ones he had made from the locust trees) and the post digger, shovel, axe and hammer, the wire stretcher, pliers, pinchers and pinch bar, an old bucket of nails and staples. . . .

That is the way Peter is, like the fellow in the gospel Jesus talks about, who says "no, no," but then goes ahead and does it anyhow; not like the fellow who says "yes, yes," but then doesn't do it.

For more than a week Peter practically went out of circulation. Whenever I would look for him or ask where he was, the answer would always be the same, "He is working on the fence."

It was one of the hottest weeks of the year, and because the heat was on Peter in several ways, he was touchy. I told him, "You don't have to take the old fence down; it would be easier if you left the old fence up and just reinforced it."

His answer was short: "There is no use leaving up that old fence; it's no good. Just leave me alone."

The neighbors began to tell me how hard Peter was working, and praising him to his face.

Then, two-thirds finished, he quit as suddenly as he had begun. I waited three weeks (it was well into July now) before I asked him when he was going to finish the fence. "That last side is good enough; I am not going to do anymore."

After a week, true to form, it happened again and this time he finished the fence all the way.

"Hurrah!" I said.

The fence, I feel, is a monument to both a father's patience and boy's growing up. Anyhow, it is time to turn the cow over to the next boy while, hopefully, Peter finds himself new and greater responsibilities in a quite different and changing world.

Is he ready? Can he make the transfer? Will the values he learned in one place hold up for him in another? Brought up in the "country," how will he face the "city"? Only time will answer these questions of a father, and by the time they are answered a father may well have passed away. But the contribution a man eventually makes, the father as well as the son, have their beginning in his own beginnings, whatever they are.

22
A Father's
Second Chance

As his teenagers try to come to terms with the world and the meaning of life for the first time, a father has to face the issues of life a second time. In a way, it is also a second chance.

It is possible to miss the second chance even more easily than the first one because the older we are the thicker is the armor of protection that we build around ourselves. Also, there is always some way, until death, of evading the issues, of jumping on the merry-go-round, of living life on the surface, of hiding. There are enough gadgets and distractions around these days to make playing at escape rather easy and endless, though obviously it doesn't lead to happiness and, if one may say so, not to reality either. And where the reality is, there the meaning also is.

Confronted by himself, by the world, and by the meaning of life during his own adolescence, a person does normally achieve a measure of maturity and a measure of adulthood. Yet, both of these things I see now as relative and never very perfect at all. There is always at least a little, if not a lot more, maturity to achieve. There is always something to be added or to be refined about one's attitude to life and one's grasp of the meaning of life. Maturity is not a static state, a high plateau with no place else to go. It too is subject to the dynamism of change—in either direction. Exposed a second time to searching and deciphering the meaning of life with his teenagers, a father may well be challenged to go up higher and to see better.

If he stays close enough and open enough to them, his teenagers will help him expose the phoniness in the world he helped to make and in the life he is living. Certainly, there is nothing mature about phoniness. Even fathers, grand as they are, are living out a lot of compromise with mammon and with the world which may have been necessary once to survive, but which can now stand a second look through the clear and uncompromising eyes of teenagers. It seems to me that this is especially true of the way daughters, with a certain innate grasp of the human, see human values more clearly.

Close personal experience is essential. It is the reason why fathers are in a unique—and sometimes enviable—position in progressively working toward fullness of maturity. If they love as fathers should, they are always in touch with the human, they are always experiencing the human through their children, through "their own flesh and blood." In short they are exposed to human life. This, as I have suggested, reaches a kind of climax and perhaps crisis during the time of their own teenagers' first working toward maturity. The exposure cuts deeply.

Not only are fathers, of all people, the most exposed, but as Peguy has said, because they are exposed, fathers are of all people the most vulnerable. This exposure, this vulnerability, is very elusive even as an insight unless one is a father. When I first read it in Peguy, it didn't touch me very deeply—though I remembered it—whereas now I feel like I might have thought of it myself. The father is exposed to all the vicissitudes of life through his children, and there are many situations in which he is as helpless as they are and can only suffer with them. He is exposed to many situations in which, during their adolescence, he is in the battle of growing up with them and can only feel with them since he cannot do for them. He faces with them the big questions of life, from their point of view, not knowing all the answers at all. He shares their doubts, some of their confusion, even some of their rebellion. For others the problem is not the same, they bring something else to it. In fact, they can even walk away from it.

Because of his exposure a father is vulnerable for several reasons. He is vulnerable first of all because for him there is no running away. He is, of all people, directly involved and there is no wiggling out of it even when there is no solution. He has taken on a burden of human beings personally, and from this burden there is no justified escape. He once was a free man who could ride off on a horse in any direction. He could tell most any situation to go to hell. But not anymore.

He is vulnerable too because now he has to listen and let the outside in—right into the living room. This is especially true when his children are bungling forward to independence. A man could almost go from his own adolescence to his death on the same set of principles and values—good, bad, or indifferent—that he achieved in the first stage of maturity, if he were not vulnerable as a father.

I really think that this exposure and vulnerability can be a kind of salvation, can lead to growth in depth, can add a new dimension. Imagine having to subject cherished principles you have come to live by, and even to swear by, to now being questioned. Why! Your very way of life manifests in a kind of epiphany what the meaning of success is! What you stand for, and have stood for, since coming to grips with reality during your own adolescence is almost a personification of the true meaning of life! But is it?

Some people can dismiss the questions because they have all the answers, but a father has a more difficult time than others dismissing them because they come to him from "his own flesh and blood." Not only that, if he does not listen and accept that the questions have value, he cannot help those who have need of his help. And so he asks himself anew: What are the things that are important in life? What is success? What am I here for? Where did I come from? Where am I going? Is there a God? And if there is, how do I love him? Am I my brother's keeper? Who was Christ? Where is he today? What is the meaning of human life in a world threatened with too much life?

The vulnerability, if nothing else, tends to set up a dialogue between a father and his children, between the everchanging new world of the son and the vanishing world of the father, between the hard line a man is prone to take in shaping the world scientifically and efficiently and the soft human touch of the daughter, serious about not merely doing something but being something fully human.

Conclusion

A<small>T THIS POINT</small> I want to say, "To be continued." I want to say this, not so much in the hope of continuing it as in the hope of being understood. Certainly this story is not finished. It does not end here. It does not, in fact, have an ending. How could it? Life goes on and lives go on, and the show does not stop for us. Whenever we take a break—to sleep, to rest, to collect our thoughts, to reflect and analyze the situation—it is not like an intermission during which the drama waits for us.

Already three years have passed since writing most of the pieces in this book, and upon reading them again in the sequence of this book I am much aware that the drama of life has not waited for me but has kept right on going. Everybody I talked about is older now. Even the half of the family I didn't talk about have kept right on growing up. All are moving forward; some are moving away. All are continuing the inevitable search for self, for meaning, for fulfillment. Sometimes, it seems that I am reaping the whirlwind, and sometimes it seems that I reap the sweet fruits of my labors. But . . .

One never knows how it will all come out. Even when science feels that it is at the point of controlling everything (Enter: rebellious youth), it seems to me that the individual is further away than ever from having things under control, even his own life. Certainly, the influences upon one's children are more manifold than ever before, so that all a father can really be sure of is that he has first chance at helping them along the way toward their very own personhood. Perhaps it is enough.

So I look at what I have written and become

aware that it is a little like yesterday's newspaper: already out of date, already behind the times. Except perhaps that . . . not having been concerned only with reporting life, but much more with searching for the meaning of human life, there is sufficient universality, sufficient applicability to everyman, sufficient common chord to have relevance for more than myself and more than yesterday.

It occurs to me further that the "vanishing world of the father" really is vanishing—not entirely out of my life, nor entirely out of the lives of my children, but the fact of its diminishing is evident. As I see it juxtaposed in this book with the new world on the horizon, I seem to become aware of its "primitive" quality, along with its peculiar simplicity and serenity. The new world into which my children are matriculating will no doubt be a better world someday, partly because the children themselves will insist on making it a better world. This is in fact the struggle going on: the children, not only mine but everyone's, are demanding not necessarily a more human world than the father's, but one which, amid a thousand new opportunities, is at least as human as home was. The concept of love is being extended to every area of life; the new opportunities must all contribute to making the world as human as a family.

If I seem to myself to have made the discovery as indicated in this book that the confrontation with his teenagers is a "growth-crisis" for the father—a real opportunity for becoming a more mature and more perfect human being—I have come to realize that something of the same is continually happening to everyone. It is the perennial problem of always making progress, of growing always, of remaining open, of becoming always more human. The task is never done for a father, teacher, everyman. If there is a serious "growth-crisis," it is only because the father, the teacher, everyman, has let himself become bogged down, has let himself accept a certain personal status quo. This can only mean losing touch, closing off, falling behind for the length of time that he does accept it.

In this connection I have come to believe and understand what my own children have taught me: that we are more mature, more human, more Christian only in terms of openness to "others," that progress in terms of ultimate values is only together with "the other." That is why we need each other, father and son, teacher and student, man and his neighbor, everyone . . . more than we have ever realized before. It is part of the new world and part of our collective leap forward in understanding ourselves better.

I also feel, on final reading, that if it all sounds "too good to be true" to anyone, then something has happened between the writing and the reading that was not intended. This is an honest book without ulterior motives. I feel the more sure of this because I really don't know why I wrote it. Maybe I did merely to find out what is just below the surface. At any rate, I never intended to write that other kind of book which dwells mainly on the miseries of life. Surely, everyone takes for granted that everything isn't always peaches and cream at our house, just as I take for granted, in that other kind of book, that everything isn't always wormwood and waste water.

The microcosm that is a big family is indeed a microcosm. It is all there. The "nitty-gritty" world is never far away. What I never hope to lose—nor my children nor anyone else may never hope to lose—is the belief in man's fundamental faith in the goodness of man.

I have said very little about God in this book. It is the season to be silent about God. But I do attest to his presence in every serious search for the meaning of life.

To be continued.

Art Notes

by Sarah Geissler

This book is very human and honest and open—
the art would have to be the same. This art I have
done is not an end in itself—I have tried to work it
so that it fits the book. In this way both the words
and the art together form the whole.

I have chosen linoleum blocks because they work
into a strong complete image. They have solidness, a
wholeness in themselves. The prints are stark, but
the result is natural, untouched and unembellished.

1) man's life, like nature, is divided into four
   seasons
2) the father-Christ image
3) the brother—second father
4) the brother—farmer, and wife
5) the brother—aged, in fall of his life

6) mother and child
7) death-sorrow—the mourning mother—the dead

child in a womb-like shape symbolizes death as a rebirth

8) father-sorrow-agony—the empty arms
9) innocent redeeming love—the parents of innocence
10) father and son

11) the reaching out and feeling of the world—the senses, a living experience of life and art
12) oldest child—water symbolizes life, a beginning
13) compassion—the hands reaching and taking—the rounded image is symbolic of completeness which is found in love
14) wedding-oneness of two figures—the young tree in the back is spring—the birth of life together
15) nature as the basis of all art—closeness of artist to it, an essential closeness
16) happiness and you—the openness of the spread hands is one with the openness of the person

17) the growing stages of the child—again, like nature
18) the rebel—a dominating figure—a cross-like figure
19) openness and giving—welcoming and reaching
20) mother and boy-child
21) a young-boy body—the beginning of a man
22) father-image—openness and acceptance

conclusion) father and children—the looking back and out upon the world